MW01107541

LIVING
BEYOND
THE PAST

Overcoming Belgium's
'Divide to Rule' Policy

INNOCENT SEZIBERA

Printed in Canada

ISBN: 978-1-4866-1430-1

Word Alive Press
131 Cordite Road, Winnipeg, MB R3W 1S1
www.wordalivepress.ca

WORD ALIVE
—PRESS—

MIX
Paper from
responsible sources
FSC
www.fsc.org
FSC® C016245

Library and Archives Canada Cataloguing in Publication

Sezibera, Innocent, author
    Living beyond the past : overcoming Belgium's divide
to rule policy / Innocent Sezibera.

Issued in print and electronic formats.
ISBN 978-1-4866-1430-1 (softcover).--ISBN 978-1-4866-1431-8 (ebook)

    1. Sezibera, Innocent. 2. Christian biography--Congo (Democratic Republic). 3. Christian biography--Canada.
I. Title.

BR1725 S49 A3 2017   276.751'083092   C2017-900211-2
                                            C2017-900212-0

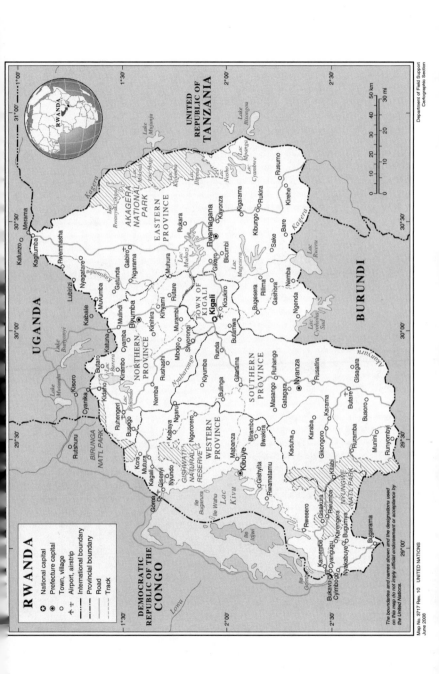

RWANDA

- ⊕ National capital
- ⊛ Prefecture capital
- ○ Town, village
- ✈ ✚ Airport, airstrip
- –··–··– International boundary
- –·–·–·– Provincial boundary
- ———— Road
- ———— Track

DEMOCRATIC REPUBLIC OF THE CONGO

UGANDA

UNITED REPUBLIC OF TANZANIA

BURUNDI

AKAGERA NATIONAL PARK

EASTERN PROVINCE

TOWN OF KIGALI

✠ Kigali

NORTHERN PROVINCE

WESTERN PROVINCE

SOUTHERN PROVINCE

BIRUNGA NATL PARK

GISHWATI NATURAL RESERVE

NYUNGWE NATL PARK

Lake Kivu

Kafunzo, Merana, Kagitumba, Rwemihasha, Nyagatare, Lubirizi, Gabiro, Ngarama, Gatunda, Mulindi, Muvumba, Kabale, Byumba, Cyamba, Katuna, Kinihira, Butaro, Kidaho, Cyanika, Kisoro, Rutshuru, Ruhengeri, Busogo, Kabaya, Ngororero, Kora, Mutura, Kagali, Gisenyi, Nyundo, Goma, Bukavu, Cyimbo, Cyangugu, Kamembe, Nyakabuye, Bugumya, Karengera, Rwumba, Gisakura, Bugarama, Rwesero, Gikongoro, Kaduha, Bwakira, Birambo, Mabanza, Gishyita, Rwamatamu, Glitarama, Bulinga, Kiyumba, Nyabarongo, Nemba, Rushashi, Mbogo, Shyorongi, Murambi, Runda, Butamwa, Ruhango, Masango, Gatagara, Karama, Nyanza, Rusatira, Gisagara, Butare, Busoro, Muniini, Runyombyi, Puramba, Karaba, Gikongoro, Rukira, Ngenda, Nemba, Gashora, Rilima, Bugesera, Kicukiro, Bicumbi, Gikoro, Rwamagana, Kayonza, Kibungo, Sake, Rukara, Rusumo, Kirehe, Bare, Ngarama, Muhura, Ritare, Kinyami, Murambi

Lake Bunyonyi, Lake Mutanda, Lake Ruhondo, Lac Burera, Lac Kivumba, Lac Muhazi, Lac Mugesera, Lac Cyohoha Sud, Lac Rwampanga, Lac Ihema, Lac Hago, Lac Mihindi, Lac Nasho, Lac Mpanga, Lac Cyambwe, Lake Mujunju, Lake Bisongou, Lac Rweru, Kagera, Kageru, Akanyaru, Nyabarongo, Akagera, Rusizi

Map No. 3717 Rev. 10   UNITED NATIONS
June 2006

Department of Field Support
Cartographic Section

| 0 | 10 | 20 | 30 | 40 | 50 km |
| 0 | 10 | 20 | 30 mi |

DEDICATION

To my wife Immaculée. The first time we met, I couldn't imagine how you would shape my manhood. Your unfailing love for me, your calmness in tough times, and your passion for ministry have made me the man I am today. I trust you without reserve.

To my three daughters (Angelique, Solange, and Yvette) and my two sons (Jonathan and Promesse). You are the best children any parent could hope for. Your self-sacrificing to the church ministry has been a source of strength to me, and an incredible inspiration to both young and old in the church and our community. Never give up.

CONTENTS

ACKNOWLEDGEMENTS

Thank you to the men and women who have given me inspiration for this book. I owe an enormous debt of gratitude to countless Hutu and Tutsi around the world who endured the animosities of the 1994 genocide, and broke the bondage of ethnic hatred. Your names may never get in print, but the example you set every day will always be remembered.

Thank you to Rev. Al Downey. You encouraged me to write this book. I appreciate the moments you took to read the book outline, and your comments that guided me through my writing.

Also, many thanks to Word Alive Press for enabling me to fulfil my dream of seeing this book published. Special thanks to Sylvia St. Cyr, my publishing consultant, and Evan Braun, my editor, for their support in all my endeavors.

Above all, I give glory and honor to God who chose me since my early age and placed before me an opportunity to share my story with His people around the world.

PREFACE

I grew up in the Democratic Republic of Congo with the fear of being killed one day because of my ethnicity. I have been named a cockroach and a snake ever since I was an innocent little boy. On the other hand, I grew up embarrassed, wondering why the Tutsi treated our neighbouring Hutu as if they were second-class citizens. I began to understand it all in my twenties, when the Rwandese Patriotic Front (RPF) attacked Rwanda on October 1, 1990.

Since then, I have read many books about the roots of the hatred between Hutu and Tutsi. Some justify the hostilities that have occurred while others create confusion and stir up constant hatred. Despite being subjected to humiliation and hatred, I never allowed my heart to build on past or present hostilities. Since my teenage years, Scripture has taught me a significant concept of life on our planet:

From one man he made all the nations, that they should inhabit the whole earth; and he marked out their

*appointed times in history and the boundaries of their
lands.* (Acts 17:26)

Therefore, as a believer, I grew up with a deep view of the
oneness of humanity beyond race, nationality, and ethnicity.
From the tower of Babel until today, the Creator moves people
from one corner of the earth to another to fulfil His purpose for
planet earth. It is up to us, especially believers, to embrace this
divine plan, whether or not it makes us comfortable.

In this book, I share my personal story of navigating the
ethnic storms in my native country, the Congo, and in Rwanda,
the country of my ancestors. I write about certain subjects that
may sound like they're meant to diminish the church, but my
intension is not to throw blame. When Paul wrote about the
apostle Peter's hypocrisy, he didn't intent to boast, nor did he
want to embarrass the apostle or the church. In the same way,
the scriptures don't cover up the sin of King David, a man
after God's own heart. Though we need wisdom and respect
for others' rights and dignity, there are times when we need to
speak for the best of our human society.

Thus, I do not pretend to be the best. Rather, by the grace
of God, I have been privileged to rise to the occasion when the
church needed brave builders. I have a deep respect for the men
and women, Hutu and Tutsi, whom God has used and is still
using to fulfil His purpose in the countries of Africa's Great
Lakes region. They are many in the church and in government.

I have shared my authentic struggles of faith and leadership.
I hope everyone reading this book will discover my deepest
longing: to live in a space where everyone can live without
prejudice towards one another due to the colour of their skin,
their ethnicity, their religion, or any other differences.

INTRODUCTION

Many books have been written about the Tutsi genocide of 1994. Filmmakers have speculated on the causes and events of the genocide that took about one million Tutsi lives in just one hundred days. The truth resides in the hearts of Tutsi and Hutu; others can only tell stories inspired by their political motivations, business opportunities, or emotions.

I was born in the Congo in the 1960s. Since my childhood, my father spoke about a potential extermination of Tutsi. I didn't know much about Rwanda; my father simply talked about our extermination in the Congo. I discovered that my parents could not share a beer, milk, or even food with a Hutu. Tutsi and Hutu could sit together and drink or eat, but a Tutsi could not drink from the same bottle, use the same straw, or eat from the same plate as a Hutu. I did not see any marriages between Tutsis and Hutus. Hutus were considered an inferior class.

At the age of twenty-five, I began to understand it all. I escaped the killings of Tutsi in the Congo, moved to Rwanda, and contributed to the rebuilding of a destroyed nation suspended between hope and uncertainty.

I lived it, I saw it, and I can tell it all. I refused to be a prisoner of ethnic hatred.

Politicians should bear the responsibility of paving a strong road of peace for the people God has placed under their leadership. Any leader promoting hatred and ethnic cleansing should first ask what legacy he intends to leave to his own children and the people he pretends to fight for. After all, in this modern world, governed by technology and sophisticated weapons, the Hutu majority cannot expect to win the battle forever. Nor can the powerful military force led by the Tutsi of Rwanda guarantee stability in the Great Lakes region. There is a need for mutual respect between the ethnic groups, and a deep understanding that Hutu and Tutsi will always live together, despite their attempts to exterminate one another.

To church leaders and dear colleagues, I have one message: has not God committed to us the word of reconciliation? When the Lord sets us free, we are free indeed. In times of deep division when the country is torn apart by internal strife, we have a duty to act as if we are in positions of influence. Otherwise, God will hold us accountable.

Chapter One

MY
CHILDHOOD

CATHOLIC PARENTS

"We picked you up in the field," my mother used to tease me. "That's why you are so dark."

I was too young to understand the kind of language, so I took it seriously and sometimes felt that I didn't belong to the family. As I grew up, I got it. I came to realize that I was a copycat of my father, and he loved me so much.

Being the seventh child in the family gave me a special place. My parents believed that my mood followed the lunar phases. If, for example, I had a bad day and it was a full moon, my family would attribute my behaviour to the lunar phase. I remember times when my parents and siblings said, "Be careful! The moon is out."

Although I was little, I was never happy about all the negative jokes and the stigmatisation. None of my parents or siblings intended to hurt me. All the jokes were allowed, although my family was Roman Catholic. My young brother and I were the only ones who weren't baptised when we were born. My parents claimed to be Catholics, although I never saw them go to mass on Sundays. They were just baptised. That was it. They started to attend a Pentecostal church after I graduated from Bible college.

My childhood development took place in the District of Rutshuru, in a small village along the border of the Congo and Uganda. Our district was located in the North Kivu province, a mountainous territory that includes a large portion of the Virunga National Park, famous for its mountain gorillas that attract tourists from around the world. The town lies in the western branch of the Albertine Rift between Lakes Edward and Kivu. The Ugandan border is fifteen kilometres east and the Rwandan border is thirty kilometres southeast. Lava flows from the Nyamuragira volcano, about forty kilometres southwest, have come within seven kilometres of Rutshuru in recent years.

The Democratic Republic of Congo (DRC) is in Central Africa and is the second largest country of the continent by area, and the eleventh largest country in the world. According to the World Bank in 2015, the Congo's population was estimated to be 77.27 million from more than 250 ethnic groups, including Tutsi and Hutu.[1] Thus, it is the fourth most populous country in Africa and the nineteenth most populous country in the world.

The DRC has the world's largest reserves of cobalt and significant quantities of diamonds, gold, copper, and other natural resources such as rivers and natural forests. This makes the DRC one of the richest countries in terms of natural resources. However, according to *Global Finance*, the DRC has become the second poorest country in the world as of 2015.[2]

---

[1] *The World Bank*, "Democratic Republic of Congo." Date of access: November 29, 2016 (http://www.worldbank.org/en/country/drc).
[2] *Global Finance*, "The Poorest Countries in the World." Date of access: November 29, 2016 (www.gfmag.com/global-data/economic-data/the-poorest-countries-in-the-world?page=12).

Also, it is the most populous francophone country. The country gained independence from Belgium on June 30, 1960. Four years later, I was born.

MY FATHER'S BOY

When I grew up, my father had significant livestock, but we didn't have a modern farm. There were open fields with pastures for common use. The herds were mixed, and herdsmen monitored the cattle. We shared our home with sheep and goats; we even had a place in our home for poultry. We were proudly rich because we always had milk to drink. Drinking water was a taboo doomed to the poor. Whenever we needed money, my father sold a cow, sheep, goat, or chicken, and the problem was solved.

Before I started school, my father carried me on his shoulders early in the morning, and sometimes in the evening, when he went to milk the cows. I was initiated as a herdsman, getting up early and spending the evenings in the open fields with my father. I was trained for the most prestigious practices of the Tutsi.

A MYSTERIOUS DISEASE

Although I was proud of my herdsman training, I envied the young people of my village who went to school. They had nice clothes, knew how to write and read, and could speak Swahili and French. My older sister and my two older brothers had stopped going to school in the elementary grades. My father had decided that my sister would stay home to help our mother with household duties, and my two brothers would look after the cattle. My other brother was in school in Grade Six, and my other sister was in Grade Two. I also had a younger brother who wasn't old enough to attend school yet.

I don't remember if I ever asked my parents to enroll me in school. However, when I was six my father enrolled me in Grade One. I still remember the excitement of going to school the first day. I was excited to meet other children from different villages, some my age and others who were older than me. We all spoke one mother tongue, Kinyarwanda, and were all one religion, Catholic. But we were either Hutu or Tutsi. We played various games together, both boys and girls, with no ethnic prejudice.

As I started to enjoy life at school, a sudden and mysterious disease cut short my dreams and ambitions. I don't know the name of the disease. Suddenly, when the dark fell at night, I couldn't see, whether there was a lamp or not. I had enjoyed playing soccer and other games under the moonlight, but after I was stricken by the disease, someone would have to lead me around. Some days I sadly sat outside until the games were over.

The disease developed quickly, to the point that I started to have difficulties reading the letters of the alphabet on the blackboard. My father decided to take me out of school. Everyone in the village knew I had left school due my disease. Many young people made fun of me by calling me *Gahuma*, meaning "blind." I wasn't happy, and neither were my relatives. I spent the rest of the school year at home.

I don't remember every effort my father made to get me healed, but there is one day I will never forget. Early in the morning, my father took me to a traditional healer who was believed to cure some types of diseases by prescribing herbal medicines. The healer wasn't able to help, but he referred me to an old woman who was well known as a specialist in traditional medicine.

As we left the healer's house, we walked about one mile and my father saw at a distance the old woman coming towards us. As we approached, my father greeted her by name. She was named Nyirabatutsi, a Hutu.

My father explained to her about my disease. She diagnosed me by looking into my eyes and prescribed a kind of herb with white sap. She then gave my father a couple of instructions in regards to administering the medication. The most important thing was that the herbs were to be kept in cold water in a covered pot. Then she prescribed some drops of the white sap into my eyes twice a day, at morning and in the evening. I didn't understand why the herbs had to be kept in cold water; we simply believed that this was part of the prescription. Now I understand that it was because no one had a fridge.

My father was a humble herdsman who didn't have a diploma or any certificate, though he had good calligraphy when he wrote letters in Kinyarwanda or Swahili. Despite his lack of education, he was well organized. He followed Nyirabatutsi's instructions, administering the medicine until I was healed.

After my healing, I started to play with my friends again under the bright moon. Later I resumed going to school. I was happy again.

A COCKROACH AND A SNAKE

The first elementary school I attended had students from Grade One to Grade Four. The Catholic school was only one mile from our home and classes were dispensed in Swahili, although the teachers explained everything in our mother tongue. From Grade One to Grade Three, all my teachers came from our extended family. My Grade Four teacher was a Hutu who was a good family friend. He loved me, and I loved him.

In September 1974, I started Grade Five at a different school five miles from our home. My teacher was a Tutsi known to beat his students when they were late in the morning or gave a wrong answer to a question. I didn't like him even though we belonged to the same ethnic group.

At the age of eleven, I started Grade Six. My teacher was a Hutu who had been born in the Congo. Several times when I passed by him, he called me a cockroach even though I was the smartest student of the class. Although I was so young, I understood that he didn't like me. If I'd had a choice, I would have moved to another school, but it was the only one close enough to our village. Despite my humiliation and discouragement, I earned the highest grade of the class at the end of the school year.

I didn't understand why the teacher gave me such humiliating nicknames until I was twenty-five, after the Rwandese Patriotic Front (RPF) launched an armed attach on the Habyarimana regime in October 1990. From then on, I understood that the nickname "Inyenzi" (cockroaches), used to describe the rebels, had something to do with the interethnic conflicts that had been happening between Hutu and Tutsi in Rwanda since 1959. According to some, the Tutsi are called cockroaches because they camouflage themselves under cover of darkness to commit crimes.

On the Inyenzi, Mary Weeks Millard writes,

During 1964 the Rwandese living in Burundi had also created a band of freedom fighters, calling themselves inyenzi (cochroaches). They linked up with Murere and the Congolese rebels. They were intent on gaining ground all the way from Burundi to Bukavu in Congo. The intention was to reach Bukavu and capture the city, which in turn would enable the inyenzi to cross the river that formed the border with Rwanda. They would then match on Cyangugu, achieving a foothold in Rwanda, so when the freedom fighters had conquered and proclaimed their independency in Rwanda, they would then invite Murere to form a Congolese government in exile with the support of the king of Rwanda. This plan failed, even with military help from Cuba and China, because Bukavu did not fall. The Inyenzi were driven back into mountainous southern region of Congo, the Shaba (Katanga) district, and were then captured.[3]

This was happening a few months before or after I was born. I knew nothing about it.

Because I didn't understand why I was named *inyenzi*, nor was I aware of the ethnic conflicts, every time my teacher called me this I spent the day feeling humiliated. He wasn't the only person who called me names based on my ethnic group, though. Too many other teachers and adults gave me nicknames characterized by extreme hatred. Other Tutsis experienced the same ill treatment.

THE FEAR OF GENOCIDE

In Grade Six, we learned about the geography of the Congo, including its provinces, natural resources, ethnic groups, and tribes. The Tutsis were not on the map. Rather, we were taught that the Tutsi were Nilotics who had come either from Ethiopia or Somalia. Our fellow Congolese called us Nilotics, Rwandans, cockroaches, and snakes to acknowledge that we were not one of them. In order words, we were aliens.

Often when we gathered for a meal or conversation before bed, my father told us to be aware of a possible attack by Hutu machetes. We lived with them, we shared the same schools,

[3] Mary Weeks Millard, *Emmanuel Kolini: The Unlikely Archbishop of Rwanda* (Colorado Springs, CO: Authentic Publishing, 2008), location 376. Kindle edition.

and I had many Hutu friends, but my father always feared that those neighbours and friends could kill us one day or burn us alive in our houses simply because we were Tutsi.

My father, a very quiet and peaceful man, had a lot to say after taking a glass of our village's traditional beer. He often spoke about a Catholic bishop who lived in Goma, a city in the Congo, as well as a politician, both planning to exterminate Tutsi.

I don't remember a time when I ever discussed this with my relatives or colleagues, but until we left the Congo in 1994 I had nightmares about people chasing me with machetes. Once I had such nightmares, it was difficult to fall asleep again.

Although I often thought about a potential genocide, I never distanced myself from my Hutu friends. There were so many more good people than bad ones. I was blessed to understand from an early age that there were good and bad people from both ethnic groups. I also grew up realizing that all Tutsi were not angels. Evil has no race or ethnicity.

Chapter Two

CALLED
TO MINISTRY

MY FIRST FOOT IN RWANDA

Despite the fear of genocide and being humiliated by teachers and neighbours, I was determined to pursue my education. I dreamed of being a medical doctor. I thought that if I became a doctor, I would have much influence and therefore could help the poor people in my village. I would fight injustice and, in due time, move my family to a European country to escape the coming genocide. North America was too far to even dream about.

Not only did I love school, I also loved sports, especially football (soccer), volleyball, and basketball. When I was in Grade Nine, in 1979, my village organized a football game between students and the villagers. I played as a right forward, or attacker. I don't remember the exact date, but I know it was before the final exams that usually took place in June. The game took place on Sunday afternoon at a school playground about one mile from my home. I had attended that school from Grades One to Four.

There were no professionals to organize or train us. People just met a few days before and designated team captains, who were deemed to be the best players. The referee was agreed upon by both sides. Players could be of any age, whether a teenager or adult. I was fifteen years old playing with adults. I was proud of that.

On that sunny Sunday, hundreds of men and women showed up to watch the game, including my father and siblings. The game began when the referee blew the whistle, after tossing a coin. Fans from both sides began to cheer.

When the first half was over, we paused for a few minutes. The referee then blew his whistle to restart the game.

In the middle of the second half, I jumped to cushion the ball, but a very tall man pushed me so hard that I missed it. I fell on my elbow, then stood up right away and pursued the ball.

A few minutes later, I felt an intense pain and couldn't move my arm. I sat down as the game continued. There were no first aid guys to look after me. Next thing I remember, my dad was beside me, trying to lift me up. I stood with his help, and he took me home.

By the time I arrived home, the pain was so intense. My mother hurried to heat water and apply a warm cloth. Despite her efforts, my pain intensified.

My family decided to take me to a clinic that belonged to a Catholic church. The clinic wasn't far, but it took several hours to get there because there was no ambulance. When we arrived, a nurse from Belgium looked at me and sent me to a hospital fifteen kilometres away. Before I left, she put a bandage on my broken arm.

When we arrived at the hospital, built and managed by Baptist missionaries from the United States, an American physician put me to sleep. When I woke up from the anaesthesia, the doctor said that my humerus was broken, but he couldn't fix it because he didn't have an artificial bone to replace it with. So he sent me to another hospital without ambulance.

We travelled for a couple of hours and arrived the next day. Dr. Rwubuzizi, a Rwandan man who had fled the country during ethnic violence, ordered his aide to get me ready for surgery. Once again I was put to sleep. When I woke up, the doctor informed me that he couldn't fix it either. Rwubuzizi, a well-known and respected physician in the district, told my sister to take me to Butare in Rwanda or Kampala in Uganda.

We returned home, feeling hopeless. As the days went by, the pain became more severe, and my chest swelled larger.

My father had a good number of cows, but he didn't have cash. Only my older brother Déo (short for Déogratias) had cash, so he and my older sister Alivera decided to take me to Rwanda for treatment. We passed through Uganda, and after two days we arrived at Ruhengeri Hospital. This was my first time setting foot on Rwandan soil. Although I didn't feel Rwandan, my pain was mixed with joy to discover the country of my ancestors.

Upon arrival, Dr. Weiss, a French surgeon, gave me hope when he said that he would perform surgery the following week. I don't remember much of what he said, but I do remember that he said I would get a few shots of penicillin to reduce my pain and stop my arm from swelling. He added that I had a few days before my chest became too swollen to stop my heartbeat, which would result in my death.

After surgery, I spent a couple weeks in hospital and then returned to my village in the Congo. For the next couple of months, I walked leaning to my right side, with bandages on my arm. I missed my final exams, and when I started to feel better a year later, I resumed Grade Nine.

MY PENTECOSTAL CHURCH IN RUTSHURU

Before I broke my arm, I had been going to catechism so that I could be baptized. Because my parents weren't regular attendees at church, I hadn't been baptized as a baby. I wanted to be a Christian and take communion; if not, my colleagues would continue to call me a pagan, which I didn't like. Also, attending mass and receiving the Eucharist was a prestige, especially for young people. After my surgery, with my arm bandaged, I didn't want to go to the mass anymore. I felt people would pity me. I felt humiliated. But I continued to have a passion for baptism to avoid being named a pagan.

One day when I was sitting in front of our house, a young man about my age who attended a Pentecostal church came to visit me. He invited me to his church, which was close to our home. I decided to go the next Sunday. At that time, I didn't know anyone with a high school education who attended that church. There were a couple Pentecostal churches in our area. When the Pentecostal Church came to the Congo in 1921, it was called Mission Libre Suedoise, or Swedish Free Mission. For people who didn't speak French, they were called the Abasaruduwaze, or the Swedish. Therefore, some called the Pentecostals Abasaruduwaze. Others, to diminish them, named them Abasazibaje, which means "new fools."

Pentecostals were ordinary people who refrained from drinking alcohol and smoking. They sang loudly and danced during their meetings, and they loved one another. The first day I attended that church, I was impressed by the sermon and the love that the men and women showed me.

The following Sunday I went back, until I finally decided to be baptized by immersion. My water baptism took place on Sunday, December 16, 1979, one week after my fifteenth birthday. Most educated people and Tutsi in my area despised the Pentecostals. I was the first young Tutsi in my area to join the church.

I always wonder if God used my arm fracture to humble me, and therefore prepare me for my future ministry. He has many ways to lead us through our destiny. He allowed Abraham to live one hundred years without a child, although He had promised him a multitude of descendants twenty-five years earlier. He is the same God who touched the socket of Jacob's hip so that his hip was wrenched as he wrestled with Him. Jacob then limped for the rest of his life. What can we say about Moses, who spent forty years in the wildness after forty years in the palace? God was preparing him to lead Israel from the Egyptian slavery. Blessed are those who were touched by the Almighty to serve His purposes.

LEAVING MY FAMILY

Despite the bandages around my neck and arm, I decided to continue my high school education. While I was in Grade Ten, I felt the call to be a full-time minister. I was already seventeen years old and my parents and relatives opposed my calling. They thought I was smart enough to be a medical doctor or someone with a big name.

Despite my young age, I decided to enrol in a Bible college at Bukavu, about four hundred kilometres from my hometown.

My journey as a Bible college student began in September 1981. I spent four years at the college. Despite my love for ministry and my success at school, I struggled to overcome the vacuum created by four years living apart from my parents and siblings. At that time, there was no modern communication, at least not in my village. Neither my family or I had access to a telephone, there was no email, Facebook, or any other social media.

The school year started in September and lasted until June. There were Christmas and Easter breaks, but I didn't always have money to visit my family. I only spent the summers with them.

In those days, students enrolled in Bible college got their school fees and other expenses covered by their respective churches. However, when I asked my home church to support me financially, the board of elders rejected my request. I was told that I wasn't eligible for financial support because I hadn't been sent by the church, although I had a letter of recommendation from the church. In order words, the board of elders selected who got to go to Bible college, and therefore only the selected ones benefited from financial support.

However, I met another student from the same church whose fees were covered even though he had enrolled the same way I had—but he was a Hutu. I hadn't met him before, because our church members were stretched over a large region of 2,709 square kilometres. The church had hundreds of chapels with thousands of members.

I completed four years at the college and had serious financial challenges. I even committed to serve the Lord in the same church that had refused to pay my school fees. I was twenty-one years old when I graduated, and I was the only Tutsi graduate in my home parish. I understood that some church leaders could have a seed of segregation. At college, I learned that even churches in South Africa and the United States had racism and segregation.

Many times when I looked back at how I had been ill-treated by my church, I was tempted to quit the ministry or move to another denomination, but I was always encouraged by Joseph's attitude. The young Hebrew had been sold as a slave by his own siblings. When he saw them almost two decades later, he treated them with love and dignity. These verses from Genesis have always been a strong pillar to my ministry, as well my daily life, in the midst of hatred, betrayal, and disappointment.

Joseph said to his brothers, "I am Joseph! Is my father still living?" But his brothers were not able to answer him, because they were terrified at his presence.

Then Joseph said to his brothers, "Come close to me." When they had done so, he said, "I am your brother Joseph, the one you sold into Egypt! And now, do not be distressed and do not be angry with yourselves for selling me here, because it was to save lives that God sent me ahead of you. For two years now there has been famine in the land, and for the next five years there will be no plowing and reaping. But God sent me ahead of you to preserve for you a remnant on earth and to save your lives by a great deliverance.

"So then, it was not you who sent me here, but God..." (Genesis 45:3–8)

You intended to harm me, but God intended it for good to accomplish what is now being done, the saving of many lives. (Genesis 50:20)

I see it as a favour to be called for a special mission in difficult times. Our Creator knows who will rise to the occasion, and therefore He prepares us ahead of time so that we will stand firm and faithfully when the time arrives.

MY ARREST

I graduated in June 1985 when I was only twenty-one years old. During my four years at college, I had the opportunity to travel to Rwanda almost every weekend. As students, we were assigned internships at a church in Bukavu (Congo) or Cyangugu, a province of Rwanda at that time. Bukavu and Cyangugu were divided by the Ruzizi River and we could walk to the border in just a few minutes. Most of the time we went to Cyangugu with other students who were a combination of Tutsi, Hutu, and Congolese. I never felt or noticed any mistreatment when I set foot on Rwandan soil.

On the other hand, I encountered discrimination in Congo. Although I had a Congolese identification card (anyone could buy one), most of the Congolese related to me as a Rwandan because of my Tutsi facial features. When I started going to Bible college in 1981, Tutsis were refused Congolese citizenship whether they were born in the Congo or not.

Rene Lemarchand writes about this in his book, *The Dynamics of Violence in Central Africa*:

> A turning point in relations between immigrant and indigenous communities came in 1981, with the adoption of a new nationality law. By a stroke of the pen the Legislative Council repealed the 1972 law that gave citizenship rights to "persons originating from Rwanda-Urundi who were residents of the Kivu before January 1, 1950," and instead adopted the notorious restrictive ordonnance-loi of March 28, 1981, which stipulated that citizenship could only be conferred on persons "who could show that one of their ancestors was a member of a tribe or part of a tribe established in the Congo prior to October 18, 1908," when the Congo formally became a Belgian colony. The dismissal of Bisengimana in 1977, for reasons that remain unclear, thus paved the way for the virtual denial of

citizenship rights to all Banyarwanda, irrespective of their date of arrival… following the promulgation of a retroactive nationality law, the Banyarwanda were for all intents and purposes denied citizenship because none could possibly meet the legal requirement of proof of ancestral residence before October 18, 1908.[4]

Despite my father's warnings about a potential genocide of the Tutsi, I travelled to Rwanda without knowing what was going on there. I had not been born yet during the mass killings in 1959, and I was too little and ignorant about politics and ethnicity to know about the killings that followed between 1964 and 1973.

After my graduation, I continued to visit Rwanda, this time the northern province of Ruhengeri and the capital of Kigali. Sometimes I travelled with my brothers who exported coffee to Rwanda. On other occasions, I travelled alone or with others to visit my brother, friends and the Pentecostal church in Ruhengeri. One of my older brothers had decided to move to Ruhengeri a few years before my graduation. He had gone there looking for employment and paid to get an identification card that marked him as a Hutu, even though he looked more Tutsi than myself. He was more aware of the ethnic inequalities in Rwanda. At the time, Hutu were more likely to get the best jobs than Tutsi.

My first ethnic incident came in 1989, one year before the Rwandese Patriotic Front (RPF) invasion. Along with my best friends, I attended a weekend wedding in Rwanda between a couple of Hutus. Many people from my home town, men and women, young and old, attended the wedding, but I was the only Tutsi. From Rutshuru, we travelled through Uganda and crossed the Cyanika border into Ruhengeri, Rwanda.

[4] Rene Lemarchand, *The Dynamics of Violence in Central Africa* (Philadelphia, PA: University of Pennsylvania, 2009), 15, 32.

The following week, on our way home, we arrived at the Cyanika border and presented our travel documents as we had upon entering the country. After a thorough inspection, everyone was cleared to travel—except me. An immigration officer put me in an isolated room for interrogation. I don't remember everything I was questioned about or what I said, but I do remember that my friends, all Hutu, refused to leave before I was released. Maybe some of them understood why I had been detained, but I didn't. I was only twenty-five years old, the youngest of the group. After a while, I was released and allowed to continue my journey to the Congo. We all thanked God for my deliverance, but we didn't discuss the possible reasons for my arrest. I personally thought that the devil simply wanted to harm me.

One year later, I understood what had happened. I had been arrested because I was Tutsi. The Tutsi, most of them living in Uganda, were about to attack Rwanda. I knew nothing about it.

Writer Allison Des Forges describes the political climate of this period:

> By the late 1980s, the Rwandan community in exile had swelled to approximately 600,000 people, most of whom lived in the countries surrounding Rwanda… In Uganda, thousands of refugees had been expelled to Rwanda in 1982, only to be pushed back again across the border shortly after. In 1986 Rwandan authorities had declared that the country was too overpopulated to permit the return of the refugees… At a meeting in Washington D.C. in 1988 Rwandans affirmed their right to return home, by force if necessary. In 1989 the Rwandan government created a commission to

deal with the refugee problem... The RPF, however, decided to go home on its own terms, proclaiming its goals to be not just the return of the refugees, but also the ouster of Habyarimana and the establishment of a more democratic government...[5]

[5] Alison Des Forges, *Leave None to Tell the Story* (New York, NY: Human Rights Watch, 1999), 48.

Chapter Three

DIVIDING
TO RULE

THE DAY I WILL NEVER FORGET

One day taught me a lot. It was the scariest day of my life, and also the day I learned how God cares for us even when we're not aware of our misfortune. Early in the morning, I heard on the radio that Tutsi had attacked Rwanda. It was October 2, 1990 and I was on a trip to Rwanda to visit some friends.

I had quickly forgotten the incident at the border, simple because I hadn't understood why I had been arrested. Rwanda and Uganda were the nearest countries to my home, and I visited often. When the news broke about the Tutsi invasion, I was riding on a bus a few miles from my hometown. I decided it wasn't necessary to get off the bus, so I continued until we arrived in Goma, a city built along Kivu Lake, just a walking distance to Gisenyi, Rwanda. I don't remember how many days I spent in Goma before returning home.

Thousands of Tutsi lived in Goma, and many of them were well informed about the situation. I met a few friends who briefed me about the Hutu resistance to the Tutsi monarchy between 1951–1960. I learned about the ethnic tensions that had resulted in the mass killing of Tutsi in 1959. More than twenty thousand Tutsis had been killed, and many more fled to the neighbouring countries of Burundi, Congo, Tanzania, and Uganda. I also learned about the Parmehutu (the party for the emancipation of the Hutu people) and the Tutsi-led UNAR (the National Rwandese Union). The killing of Tutsi continued in 1964, and again in 1973, each time causing thousands of survivors to flee Rwanda. Later I learned about the same ethnic conflicts that had been going on between the Hutu and Tutsi in Burundi.

I was twenty-six years old when I learned about the conflicts between Hutu and Tutsi. When I returned to my hometown, I kept hearing the news on the BBC, France-Inter, Voice of America, and local media: Tutsi were being arrested and killed in Rwanda. A few months later, thousands of refugees from Rwanda, all Tutsi, arrived in our area. Allison Des Forges describes the government response to the attack three days after:

> The attack offered Habyarimana the opportunity to rebuild his eroding base of power by rallying Rwandans against the enemy. In response to the news, the great majority of people, Tutsi and Hutu opponents of the regime included, came to the support of the government... Rather than rely on a spontaneous coalescing support from all sides, Habyarimana decided to pursue a more forceful strategy, to sacrifice the Tutsi in hopes of uniting all Hutu behind him. On October 4, the RPF had advanced a considerable distance into Rwanda but was still forty-five miles from Kigali. That night, however, heavy firing shook the capital for several hours. In the morning the government announced that

the city had been attacked by RPF infiltrators who had been driven back by the Rwandan army. Under the pretext of assuring security, the government began making massive arrest in Kigali and elsewhere in the country, eventually imprisoning some 13,000 people. The detainees would be held without charge, thousands of them months, in deplorable conditions. Many were tortured and dozens died… In fact, the attack had been faked. Habyarimana staged the event to have credible grounds for accusing Tutsi of supporting the enemy.[6]

Had I been in Rwanda prior to October 1, even a few hours before the RPF attack, who knows if I would have survived?

THE ETHNIC CONFLICTS

As ethnic tensions intensified in Rwanda, its waves reaching us in the Congo, I wanted to understand more about the real problem. The friends' briefing in Goma and the news wasn't enough to make me understand why humans could live with such animosity. Hutu and Tutsi had spoken the same language for a thousand years, had same culture, and the majority were Christian.

Author Will Ferguson writes,

By the time the genocide began, Rwanda was the most Christianized country in Africa. Fully 90 percent identified themselves as Christians, and of these, 65 percent belonged to the Catholic Church. Hutus and Tutsis went to the same Sunday services, sat on the same pews, sang from the same hymnals.[7]

---

[6] Ibid., 49.

[7] Will Ferguson, *Road Trip Rwanda: A Journey into the Heart of Africa* (Toronto, ON: Penguin Group, 2015), 103.

Why then such deep hatred between brethren? I needed answers, and my curiosity opened a door to search for more truth. As the years passed, I got a glimpse of what had been happening ever since the Europeans had arrived in Rwanda. I was deeply shocked to find out that our misfortune had been created and strengthened by outsiders. Reliable sources affirm that all three groups—Hutu, Tutsi, and Twa—lived together for centuries without fatal conflicts.

Bishop Rucyahana has taught me a lot in his book *The Bishop of Rwanda*. With respect to his long experience and deep knowledge of the Rwandan history, I have quoted below his description of our misfortune.

The history of Rwanda not only provides clear insight into the causes of the genocide, but also gives a good perspective on the roots of the struggles we face in modern-day Africa. A few nations have benefited from colonization, but in most cases the damage far outweighs any benefit. The Germans colonized Rwanda in 1897, and were content with a loose, indirect rule. When the Belgians took mover in 1916, after World war I, things remained pretty much the same until their active colonization policy was implemented in 1921.

At that time there were three ethnic groups living in Rwanda: the Hutu made up about 80 percent of the population, the Tutsi just under 20 percent, and the Twa less than 1 percent. All three groups lived in relative peace. It would be wrong to say that Rwanda was a land of peace and idyllic harmony, but there was no trace of systematic violence between the Tutsi and Hutu. There were many wars, but they pitted what was called the

Banyarwanda as a group against foreign nations or tribes. This is not to say there wasn't occasional fighting between the local chiefs, but there was no such thing as a universal Hutu-versus-Tutsi animosity. They were considered equals, they intermarried, they served in the same army, and they were in the service on the same king. It is true that the king was a Tutsi, but they were many chiefs—both Hutu and Tutsi. The king had Hutu wives as well as Tutsi wives. He had Tutsi servants as well as Hutu servants.

The question is how—after living together in virtual peace for hundreds of years—did such a murderous hatred arise... The sad truth is that this hatred was created and manipulated by the Belgian colonial masters to make the people easier to control. Our nation was much larger than it is today, and the Rwandan king was powerful. He had a solid administration and an economy that worked. He had power and the communication to keep it.

The first thing the Belgians did was weaken the kingdom by attaching a large piece of it to the Congo, where they had firmer control. This deprived the kingdom of many of its subjects. Then they attached another parcel of land to Uganda, and Rwanda became even smaller. It would now be impossible for the king to regroup his people and rebel against the Belgian rule.

The Belgians still felt it necessary to have divisions in a country where everyone lived together and spoke the same language. If there were no natural divisions they could use, the colonial masters were not above creating them. As soon as the Belgians took power, they decided to favor the Tutsi over the Hutu and began placing the Tutsi taskmasters over their Hutu countrymen.[8]

Alison Des Forges provides more insight:

Once the Belgians had decided to limit administrative posts and higher education to the Tutsi, they were faced with the challenge of deciding exactly who was Tutsi. Physical characteristics identified some, but not for all. Because group affiliation was supposedly inherited, genealogy provided the best guide to a person's status, but tracing genealogies was time-consuming and could also be inaccurate, given that individuals could change category as their fortunes rose or fell. The Belgians decided that the most efficient procedure was simply to register everyone, noting their group affiliation in writing, once and for all. All Rwandans born subsequently would also be registered as Tutsi, Hutu, or Twa at the time of their birth. The system was put into effect in the 1930s, with each Rwandan asked to declare his group identity.[9]

As I continued to search for the roots of the ethnic conflicts between Hutu and Tutsi, I also had a deep understanding about who were the "Banyarwanda" of Congo. According to Lemarchand, the so-called Banyarwanda included three groups.

---

[8] John Rucyahana with James Riordan, *The Bishop of Rwanda* (Nashville, TN: Thomas Nelson, 2007), location 178–195. Kindle edition.
[9] Alison Des Forges, *Leave None to Tell the Story* (New York, NY: Human Rights Watch, 1999), 37.

(a) Hutu and Tutsi who had settled in the Kivu region (east of Congo) long before the advent of colonial rule, including a group of ethnic Tutsi indigenous to south Kivu (located in the Mulenge region) known as Banyamulenge; (b) descendants of migrant workers, mostly Hutu, brought in from Rwanda in the 1930s and 1940s under the auspices of the colonial state; (c) tens of thousands of Tutsi refugees who fled Rwanda in the wake of the 1959 Hutu revolution.[10]

---

[10] Rene Lemarchand, *The Dynamics of Violence in Central Africa* (Philadelphia, PA: University of Pennsylvania, 2009), 32.

Chapter Four

PASTORING
IN THE CONGO

OUR WEDDING

Although I was often called a cockroach and a snake, and despite my father's prediction of a Tutsi genocide, there was no real threat of our extermination in the Congo until the RPF invaded Rwanda on October 1, 1990. Since then, many young men, mostly Tutsi, joined the RPF to combat the Habyarimana regime.

One month after the RPF attack, a dozen pastors laid their hands on me and I became the first unmarried pastor in the largest Pentecostal denomination in the Congo. However, during the following months and years I was called an *inyenzi inkotanyi*, to identify me with the Tutsi rebels.

Despite the discrimination I had experienced, I didn't allow any situation to prevent me from working hand in hand with the Hutus. Spending four years at Bible College gave me the opportunity to understand that the prince of this world uses all sorts of tactics to arouse hatred to destroy brethren. Time and again, the sons of Jacob (the Israelites) turned against one another until the holy land was divided into two kingdoms after the death of King Solomon. Before I went to the Bible college, I witnessed my uncle chase his son with a spear, wanting to kill him. In my own village, relatives fought fiercely against one another when they were drunk, or when they were unable to compromise about how to share family property.

Thus, when the day of my own wedding approached, in the midst of severe ethnic tensions, I solicited a Hutu pastor to perform the ceremony. His wife was Hutu also and she was my wife's bridesmaid. My best man was a Hutu pastor. Most of the people from my village, as well as other Tutsis, were offended. However, my wife Immaculée and I were extremely joyful on that blessed day of March 1991, because we were surrounded by God's servants, not Hutus. As Christians, we need to stand tall and proudly display the values that portray who we are.

Immaculée and Innocent's wedding in March 1991.

Ever since I was fifteen, I attended churches with a Hutu majority. They were my spiritual brothers and close friends. We worshipped together, prayed and fasted together, and helped one another whenever we could. I refused to be a prisoner of my ethnicity, though many thought I lacked judgment and family values. I lived what I believed about the cross, that Jews and Gentiles were one in our Lord and Saviour Jesus Christ. That is my faith. That is my identity.

THE CAMPAIGN AGAINST THE TUTSI OF CONGO

As Immaculée and I enjoyed life and hoped to hold our first baby in a few months (we didn't know if it was a boy or a girl), ethnic tensions interfered with our future. The more progress the RPF made, the more tensions between Hutu and Tutsi intensified.

In the Congo, a group of Hutu called MAGRIVI (Mutuelle Agricole des Virunga) was founded in 1989. The MAGRIVI began a hatred campaign against Tutsi across the country, especially in Rutshuru, Goma, and Masisi. The districts of Rutshuru and Masisi, and the city of Goma were the areas with the highest population of Hutu and Tutsi. There were also the Banyamulenge, a group of Tutsi in the Kivu South province, but there were no Hutu communities there. The Banyamulenge lived about four hundred kilometres from the town where we lived. Therefore, they were not targeted as enemies of Rwanda, although they were also discriminated against and sometimes identified as Rwandans.

The only hope for Tutsi in Congo was God, who used the former president Mobutu to protect us. He was a corrupt leader and made Congo the poorest country in the world (he assassinated fellow politicians), but he protected the Tutsi minority. If Mobutu had allowed the MAGRIVI militants to do whatever they wanted, they would have massacred the Tutsi of Congo before the 1994 genocide in Rwanda.

The MAGRIVI ideology of hatred was so deep in people's minds. I will never forget an incident that happened one Sunday after I preached about Moses' faith in a chapel in Rutshuru a few months before the Tutsi genocide. I delivered a sermon on Hebrews 11:24–27:

> By faith Moses, when he had grown up, refused to be known as the son of Pharaoh's daughter. He chose to be mistreated along with the people of God rather than to enjoy the fleeting pleasures of sin. He regarded disgrace for the sake of Christ as of greater value than the treasures of Egypt, because he was looking ahead to his reward. By faith he left Egypt, not fearing the king's anger; he persevered because he saw him who is invisible.

Note what the Hebrews writer says: *"He chose to be mistreated along with the people of God..."* In Kinyarwanda, my mother tongue, the word people is translated as *ubwoko*, which has a connotation of tribe or ethnicity. As far as I remember, there was no other Tutsi in the audience; I was the only one. Most Tutsi were Roman Catholics.

While I was preaching on Moses' faith, as any preacher would, many from the audience perceived me as a Tutsi expressing my plans to join the RPF to fight the Hutu regime in Rwanda. Up to this time, I was proud to be Congolese. My wife and I had never before thought to move to Rwanda.

After my sermon, I went back home thinking the congregation had been blessed by the sermon. A few weeks later, our senior pastor called me into his office to discuss my plans to join my brothers' fight in Rwanda. In the beginning, I didn't understand what he was talking about, but then he explained how I had said in my sermon that I hated Congo, and therefore I was going to join the fight against the Hutu regime in Rwanda.

The senior pastor hadn't been present when I delivered my sermon. He was overseeing a large local church with hundreds of chapels. No doubt, someone had told him about my so-called plans and he wanted to know my side of the story.

After that, I began to understand that things were more serious than I'd thought. Thus, despite my passion for ministry, there came a time when I felt like I didn't belong to that church, nor to my native country. My love for the ministry was mixed with uncertainty. However, I continued my ministry faithfully, not knowing what awaited us.

The MAGRIVI militants became very dangerous between 1992 and 1994. One day a pastor from our local church, a long-time friend of mine, said in front of me during suppertime that he slept with a machete underneath his pillow. That night, he argued that the *inkotanyi* could strike our area at any time, and therefore he was ready to protect himself and his family.

Every time I remember his argument, I visualize the apostle Peter walking with a sword before he was transformed by the Holy Spirit on the day of Pentecost. My fellow pastor's comments didn't surprise me; any carnal leader can do anything, especially in countries where human rights are not respected.

Robert Garretó, a UN reporter in the Congo (formerly Zaire), made the following report describing the MAGRIVI in North Kivu:

> Besides the problem of power and nationality which sets the Banyarwanda against the "original" ethnic groups, there is a dispute within the Banyarwanda between Tutsis and Hutus, which has been exacerbated by the inter-ethnic conflict in Rwanda and Burundi.

Concerned at their lack of power, the Banyarwanda have decided to venture into politics. Although for the most part they are Hutus, the person who has attained the highest office is Barthelemi Bizengimana, a Tutsi who rose to be the director of Marshal Mobutu's cabinet. Tutsis are more strongly represented than Hutus in the former Parliament, the National Sovereign Conference and the current Supreme Council of the Republic-Transitional Parliament.

Finding themselves outweighed politically and economically by their Tutsi brethren, the Hutus formed a variety of groups, most notably the Virunga Farmers and Herders Association (Mutuelle des Agriculteurs et Eleveurs du Virunga (MAGRIVI)) founded in 1989 by, among others, Sekimonyo wa Magango, the current Minister for Higher Education and Scientific Research, which was given strong backing by President Habyarimana's regime in Rwanda. The Special Rapporteur has been told that, starting in 1992, the Association sold farm produce to invest in weapons and took part in the 1994 genocide…

The Special Rapporteur was told that MAGRIVI, whatever its original welfare or cultural objectives, has changed or been consolidated into a militia bent on winning power for the Hutus and has worked closely with the Interahamwe (those who attack together). In the long run its objective is to establish a Hutuland, a racially pure area dominated by Hutus.

One day, Immaculée and I, with our one-year-old daughter Angelique, spent a night in the bush behind our house. During the day, we had heard that the MAGRIVI militants planned to kill us with machetes or burn us alive. I don't recall how we got the information, but we weren't killed that night! Although we lived in the Congo, and despite Mobutu's efforts to calm the situation, we continued to breathe the fear of genocide.

My father's prediction of an imminent genocide was becoming more evident. The warning signs were clear in Rwanda. We in the Congo feared that we would be killed at any time.

THE DEATH OF TWO PRESIDENTS
While the MAGRIVI was enough to shake our lives in the Congo, another misfortune occurred. At dawn on Thursday, July 7, 1994, a young man knocked at our bedroom door. Prince was a student who had come from the Banyamulenge region a few months earlier to study at a new university in Rutshuru. The university was about two miles from our home, and a friend of Prince's family had asked us to accommodate him during his studies. Prince's voice trembled when he spoke. "Pastor, let us flee right now."

I woke up very sleepy, wiping my eyes. "What's going on, Prince?

"Let us flee," he said in a terrified voice. "Habyarimana and Ntaryamira are dead."

I thought Prince was out of his mind, and I asked him to calm down. But he kept going, adding that RFI (Radio France Internationale) had just announced that President Habyarimana of Rwanda and President Ntaryamira of Burundi had died in a plane crash at Kigali airport.

I held my breath. "Calm down," I told him. "We won't die. Only the Tutsi in Rwanda will be exterminated."

This spontaneous response wasn't a prophecy but a rationale of everything I had heard since my childhood.

My wife, Angelique, our second daughter Solange (born two months prior to the plane crash), Prince, and I stayed in the living room that day searching for more news on the radio station. Sadly, all we heard in the following hours and weeks was about more killing of Tutsi and moderate Hutu in Rwanda. Every evening I turned on the BBC, RFI, or the Voice of America and heard that the killings were intensifying. As the RPF made progress, more and more Hutu fled the country. Others were killed by bullets while fleeing the fighting. By the end of July 1994, there were thousands of refugees in Rutshuru. They were everywhere on the streets, in school playgrounds, and in churches. Our church had built a high school with a huge playground surrounded by trees. Hundreds of refugees camped along our compound and the playground. Every time my wife and I went out, we passed through hundreds of refugees chatting, making food for themselves, and taking care of little ones. The anguish and bitterness was clear on their faces.

Almost one week after the refugees were settled down in our backyard, we couldn't sleep anymore. Among the refugees were Rwandan soldiers, still with their guns. We also heard that some were *interahamwe*, the militias that had helped the army to kill Tutsis. Immaculée and I feared we could be killed any moment. Around this time, our second daughter, Solange, was four months old. Angelique was already two and a half years.

Immaculée and I started to discuss whether we should move, but it was a difficult decision. We had both been born in the Congo. In our area, hundreds of Hutu refugees were falling ill and dying from cholera, and there was a strong propaganda that the Tutsi had poisoned their water. Being Tutsi, our neighbours said that my wife and I were in league with accomplices.

Before the refugees arrived, families in our church would gather for evening meals. Everyone involved in ministry brought food to our senior pastor's dining room, and all the men ate together. Women had their supper in the kitchen. The last week before we left Congo, things changed dramatically. My colleagues refrained from bringing food at the regular table. They decided to use another house for supper without letting my wife and I know. Neighbour children used to come into our house to eat whatever was available, but not anymore.

One night, our senior pastor approached me and Immaculée with frustration on his face. He then told us that he had overheard evil plans against us, and he advised us to leave as soon as we could. That night, I don't remember the exact day, we planned our escape. The senior pastor suggested that his wife and daughter would wake early in the morning and help us carry our luggage. The plan was for Immaculée, our two daughters, and I would leave in the dark and catch a taxi to Uganda. Our senior pastor was a Hutu, but he was a very close friend of mine and didn't want us to lose our lives. When other pastors withdrew from our dining table, he continued to support us and told us secretly what was going on.

Early in the morning, when the sky was still dark, the senior pastor came to our house with his wife and daughter. All night, Immaculée and I had packed clothes. We handed a bag to the daughter and left first, under cover of dark, accompanied by the senior pastor. His daughter and wife met us later at the bus station. There was no bus, so we caught a ride on a pickup truck that was heading to the Ugandan boarder. The driver started the truck and the pastor and his family waved goodbye to us with sadness.

We travelled about one hour and reached the Ugandan border safely.

Two years later, although the Congo was not safe, I went back to Rutshuru to find out how the senior pastor and his family were doing after these days of war. He passed away before we met again. I hope to meet him in heaven when my days on earth are over. There, there won't be Hutu or Tutsi.

Chapter Five

A NEW LIFE IN
RWANDA

A REFUGEE ON MY ANCESTOR'S LAND

I had always visited Uganda frequently. My uncles, aunts, cousins on my mother's side lived in Uganda. When the truck dropped us off at the Ugandan boarder, I knew which way to take to avoid both the Congolese and Uganda immigration forces. We had left Rutshuru in a hurry hadn't had time to apply for travel documents. Therefore, it would have been difficult to cross the border. We spent a couple of hours monitoring the situation, and in the end we managed to escape the immigration officers from both sides.

As we put our feet on Ugandan soil, my wife and I decided to spend a few days at my aunt's place. I don't remember how many days we stayed there before we decided to continue to Cyanika on the Rwandan border, where I had been arrested five years earlier. On our way to Rwanda, our big puzzle was how to survive in a country torn by a war that had lasted four years and killed about a million Tutsis.

Despite thousands of questions and plenty of uncertainty, we continued our journey and finally arrived at the border.

We didn't have any trouble crossing. The immigration officers assumed we were Rwandans returning from the exile.

A young Tutsi lady welcomed us. Despite her soft words and niece smile, she thoroughly screened our luggage to make sure we didn't have any weapons. After doing her job, she looked at me and said, "You have nice clothes." Then she let us continue our journey.

Our feet were already in Rwanda, but we didn't feel any joy to settle in the land of our ancestors. Rather, my wife and I kept talking about how we were going to live in Rwanda without housing, money, or employment.

We arrived in Kidaho, a short distance from the border, where many returnees from the Congo were camping. There was no housing or tents. We didn't see the UNHCR (United Nations High Commissioner for Refugees) or the Red Cross. There were only returnees.

As the night fell, we slept on green grass under the stars, surrounded by RPF soldiers. It was July, a dry season with no rain. We all spoke Kinyarwanda, and everyone was nervous about the future. None of us had a clear plan of where and how to start a new life.

Amid all the confusion, we got news that in the city of Ruhengeri, fifteen kilometres away, people could find free housing. That's where I had gotten surgery fifteen years earlier, and where my friend had gotten married.

I left Immaculée and our two little daughters and took a minibus to Ruhengeri. When I arrived, I met a close friend who helped me to find a house suitable for my family. This friend had arrived from the Congo a few weeks earlier and was already settled in a beautiful house. These houses had been left by Rwandese fleeing the country after the RPF took power. Other houses belonged to Tutsi families who had been decimated by the genocide.

I returned to Kidaho to bring my family. As soon as I arrived in the camp, I told my wife about the house. The next morning, we left the camp and settled in Ruhengeri.

As we started our new life in Rwanda, my wife and I became more concerned about the future. Although we had a temporary house, we needed money for food and other daily needs. It was bearable for me and Immaculée to spend a day without food, but it was not so for Angelique and Solange. Either they had something to eat or drink, or they wouldn't stop crying. We continued to struggle until we got some money that helped my wife start a small business at a public market. She didn't get much, but we at least had enough for daily bread.

Now that I've moved to Canada, I often wonder how the hundreds of thousands of returnees survived in Rwanda in those first years of settlement. For us living in developed countries, whether we are employed or not, it's easy to find food, housing, education, and healthcare. Though we may not have everything we need, we can at least survive with the little we get from employment insurance, savings, credit cards, etc. In Canada, there are even food banks and other charities that provide clothing, meals, and bus tickets. That's not always the case in other countries. When we arrived in Rwanda in 1994, there were no such programs to help us transition.

However, two thousand years ago Jesus Christ, the Son of God, taught His disciples the secret of life. As the Twelve followed him day and night, they didn't have time to make money for their daily living. They probably worried much. Jesus, knowing their thoughts, addressed their concerns. The following is the apostle Matthew's record of Jesus teaching on this life:

Therefore I tell you, do not worry about your life, what you will eat or drink; or about your body, what you will wear. Is not life more than food, and the body more than clothes? Look at the birds of the air; they do not sow or reap or store away in barns, and yet your heavenly Father feeds them. Are you not much more valuable than they? Can any one of you by worrying add a single hour to your life?

And why do you worry about clothes? See how the flowers of the field grow. They do not labor or spin. Yet I tell you that not even Solomon in all his splendor was dressed like one of these. If that is how God clothes the grass of the field, which is here today and tomorrow is thrown into the fire, will he not much more clothe you— you of little faith? So do not worry, saying, "What shall we eat?" or "What shall we drink?" or "What shall we wear?" For the pagans run after all these things, and your heavenly Father knows that you need them. But seek first his kingdom and his righteousness, and all these things will be given to you as well. Therefore do not worry about tomorrow, for tomorrow will worry about itself. Each day has enough trouble of its own. (Matthew 6:25–34)

Though life was so hard during our first years in Rwanda, God provided our needs.

A COLD WELCOME

Beside our need for shelter, food, and other necessities, we also needed a place of worship. A Pentecostal church was located within a ten-minute walk of our home, so we started to attend the church regularly. A few years earlier, I had preached there when I was in the city for a visit. Some in the church who survived the war still remembered me. Unfortunately, the senior pastor and district overseer, who knew me well, had fled the country. Because I was a Pentecostal pastor from the Congo, I had hoped to have a warm welcome from the fellow pastors and Christians I met.

As the days passed, two other pastors joined us —one from Uganda, another from Congo. Instead of the warm welcome we expected, some brothers and sisters associated us with the *inkotanyi* (RPF fighters who had overthrown the Hutu regime). We heard it many times, but we tried to calm ourselves. I understood that people were still under the trauma of the war. The anguish was still visible on almost every face.

While we thought about our ministry and the fellow Christians who had come from various countries, we didn't think much about the crisis that the Pentecostal church in Rwanda was going through. ADEPR (L'Association des Eglises de Pentecote du Rwanda) had been started in Rwanda in 1940 by Swedish missionaries. Statistics from 1993, which I saw in the ADEPR office in 1996, show that the denomination had about 230,000 members across the country, with more than a hundred elementary schools, two high schools, a Bible college, and a medical centre, all achieved in partnership with Sweden. When we arrived in Rwanda, the majority of the executive committee members, including the legal representative and his deputy, had fled the country. Now the church was led by an interim committee composed of the Hutu. The previous executive committee had also been composed by the Hutu and had operated from Nairobi in Kenya, giving instructions to the interim committee.

Things worsened when we were refused to partake of Holy Communion. In the Pentecostal churches in the Congo and Rwanda, Holy Communion took place one Sunday a month at the end of the service. Usually, those who hadn't been baptized by immersion and guests without a letter of recommendation from their pastors were directed to leave the sanctuary before communion began. Then, deacons passed through the congregation to make sure everyone was a member of the church. If they found a non-member, they asked him or her to leave or provide a letter of recommendation before he or she was welcomed to partake of Holy Communion. After a few times partaking, we were told that a decision was made to stop us from joining. In order words, we were not recognized as members of the ADEPR. The announcement was made in each local Pentecostal church across the country.

Some of us began to think we should join other churches that seemed more welcoming, or start new churches. There were many reasons to avoid existing churches. The majority of them were led by Hutu pastors and made up of mostly Hutu members. With fresh memories of the genocide, some Tutsi returnees didn't wish to speak or even look at the Hutu. But we Christians had different values. Despite the genocide and cold welcome, we continued to feel that we were one in Jesus Christ. The life of Joseph continued to inspire me to show patience and love toward both the Hutu and Tutsi in our Pentecostal church.

One day, in the midst of ethnic tensions, I travelled from Ruhengeri to Kigali. I was going to visit a former soldier and well-educated man who had gotten his military training in France and served in the Rwandan Army during the Hutu regime. He was a Hutu, known to be moderate, and a man of God who never hid his Christian beliefs. Someone had told me about him, and I wanted to meet him. When I arrived at his home, he was not there.

A friend of mine whom I had met in Kigali then took me to the place where the former lieutenant of the Rwandan Army was holding a small prayer meeting. The lieutenant didn't know me, and I didn't know him either. My friend and I entered the house where they were still kneeling for prayer. We joined the prayer without interrupting.

As soon as the prayer meeting was over, an old woman surprised me. I was a Tutsi, she was a Hutu, and we had never met before. The old woman looked at me and asked, "Are you a pastor?"

"Yes," I answered.

"God is calling you to big responsibilities, but you are looking back."

I didn't understand what she meant. However, being familiar with prophetic messages, I kept her words in my heart.

A few days later, like Joseph, I had a dream that confirmed her prophecy. I was reminded once again that God has no preference of ethnic group, race, or gender. Why had the prophecy come from the mouth of an old Hutu woman in the midst of ethnic tensions? I understood more than ever that God could still bring Hutu and Tutsi together in harmony in the Pentecostal church of Rwanda.

Afterwards I had a conversation with the former soldier, Lieutenant Andre, and then I returned to Ruhengeri. Andre, a long-time member of the Pentecostal church, later initiated a dialogue between the church interim committee and pastors who had returned from Burundi, Congo, and Uganda. The interim committee appointed a small group of pastors to represent those from the diaspora. I was one of the few pastors selected to attend the dialogue.

The dialogue continued over several occasions without reaching a compromise. Andre understood the country's laws, and he knew that the Pentecostal church didn't have a legal leadership at the national level. The church president, his assistant, and the majority of the executive committee had fled the country. According to law, the general assembly was to elect an executive committee which was approved by the government through a Prime Minister's Order, published in the Official Gazette of the Republic of Rwanda.

Andre tried to forcefully negotiate the leadership of the Pentecostal church, but it took me a while to understand his manipulative plan. I didn't know much about Rwanda, nor did I understand much of church politics. I had just come from the Congo a short while ago.

In the end, I realized that Andre was using military strategies by pretending to advocate for the Tutsi pastors and thousands of members who had returned from exile. Therefore, I distanced myself from him. Later, the police arrested him for stirring up tensions in the Pentecostal church across the country. After consultation with the interim committee, on June 20, 1996, the government of Rwanda appointed a legal transition committee to organize elections in order to put in place a legal executive committee at the national level. I was appointed secretary of the committee. The government gave us a one-year term to organize elections.

When the Prime Minister's Order came out with my name in the Official Gazette, I understood clearly the old woman's prophecy. However, I didn't understand immediately what it meant for me to coordinate activities of a church that had been torn by ethnic tensions after four years of a war that culminated in genocide. There were already three hundred thousand church members across the country, more than a hundred elementary and high schools to rehabilitate, and many more activities.

When news of my appointment went out by word of mouth and through the radio, many friends came to congratulate me. One thing annoyed me, though. Only Tutsi congratulated me for my new role. Many expressed their excitement for winning the battle. They saw my appointment as a victory over the Hutu. My perspective was different. From the beginning, I understood that I had not been appointed to serve the Tutsi. I was there for the Pentecostal church to serve hand in hand with everyone to bring healing to a wounded, divided people. As young as I was, I began my duties with high expectations from some, and disappointment from others.

Chapter Six

MY LEADERSHIP
JOURNEY

LEADING DURING DEEP ETHNIC TENSIONS

In 1996, thousands of Rwandans were still returning home from countries around the world. Great multitudes returned from Burundi, Congo, Uganda, and Tanzania where they had lived for at least three decades. They were Christians, Muslims, and non-religious. They kept coming in multitudes even though they had no relatives in Rwanda, no housing, and no employment. Life was precarious, especially for families with children. The returnees met most often in churches. They had spiritual needs, but they also had daily living needs, and many churches weren't prepared to assist these newcomers.

On the other hand, Hutu refugees had also fled the country when the RPF overthrew the genocidal government in July 1994. About two million had fled to the Congo. They set up camps in Eastern Congo from which militants launched attacks on Rwanda. Rwanda launched a return attack that forced many refugees to come home. Many returned to their previous churches. I was there as the secretary of the largest Pentecostal denomination in East and Central Africa.

Prior to my appointment, I had been exposed to ethnic tensions. However, I had never been at such a high position. Not only was the position new and challenging in nature, it also required experience in conflict resolution. The trauma of the genocide was present in everyone's minds, both Hutu and Tutsi. Every church in Rwanda had three distinct groups: the Hutu, the Tutsi survivors of the genocide, and the Tutsi who had returned from the diaspora. Each group had its own issues. The majority of the Hutu carried the guilt of the genocide and feared revenge from the Tutsi now in power. Others among them had lost family members during the genocide. Many more had been separated from relatives who had fled to other countries when the previous government fell and the RPF took power. The second group, the Tutsi survivors, were traumatized from the genocide. Many of them had lost people and properties, and the physical and psychological scars were still fresh. Many of us from outside Rwanda had little to give to either Hutu or Tutsi survivors. We had our own struggles.

I was on the transition committee, the only one from the diaspora, and I was the youngest of them at twenty-nine years old. Pastor Jean Sibomana, the president of the executive committee, was a Hutu in his forties. He had been born and raised in Rwanda. Pastor Justin Gasana, the vice-president, was a Tutsi is his fifties, a survivor of the genocide. Vedaste Gasangwa, the treasurer, was in his forties and also a Tutsi survivor of the genocide; he was married to a Hutu wife and was a close friend of Sibomana. From the beginning, many people in the denomination thought Swedish missionaries and the Sibomana circle had chosen Vedaste for the transition committee to silence me, and he attempted to do so several times until he realized that I wasn't there to fight. All my three colleagues lived in the country before and during the genocide. They understood better than me the social and political issues ahead of us.

A short while after my appointment, we had our first business meeting. My three colleagues knew one another and I didn't. They all spoke without accent, and I spoke with a Congolese accent. But I knew every word in Kinyarwanda. I also understood every proverb in my mother tongue. However, there was one thing I did not understand. Millard summarizes it in a few words:

> Openness of spirit is not the norm in the traditional Rwandese culture in which people prefer to keep their secrets to themselves. It could be a work of God through His Spirit that would break down such barriers between people, allowing them to begin to trust each other, no matter from which ethnic group they originated.[11]

A great task awaited us, but in the beginning we spent more time playing with words.

During our first meetings, I spoke openly about the ethnic tensions that were tearing up the church and the country, but my colleagues wouldn't comment much on my opinions. They knew more than I did. Finally, I realized that each of them had been affected by the horrifying events that had shaken the whole country, although they didn't talk openly about it. They were all victims. I was too hurried to fix things and move forward, but my colleagues were hurt and also needed to heal progressively. Although I was horrified by the genocide, I wasn't so deeply affected as the Hutu and the Tutsi of Rwanda who had lived

[11] Mary Weeks Millard, *Emmauel Kolini: The Unlikely Archibishop of Rwanda* (Colorado Springs, CO: Authentic Publishing, 2008), 163.

it. I didn't get it completely. The Swedish missionaries who had partnered with the Pentecostal church in Rwanda since 1940 didn't get it either.

Afterwards, I understood that I was there to keep the balance in the team. We only had a one-year term to put in place an elected executive committee, and the time was passing quickly. Every one of us felt the pressure to get the work done. The task was so big.

We began to build trust between us, and then we committed to visiting local churches across the country. There were more than two hundred local churches, most in rural areas. At ever church, we first had a service with the whole congregation, and afterwards we met with pastors and elders. The Hutu were always the majority, whether it was a service or a business meeting.

In the meetings with pastors and elders, the ethnic tensions were so clear. In some cases, Tutsi complained about Hutu pastors who had betrayed their church members during the genocide, or who had been involved in the killings. Hutu complained about Tutsis who falsely accused Hutu pastors, elders, and church members of being *interahamwe* (the Hutu militias that had perpetrated the genocide). In the Pentecostal church in the Congo, I had faced ethnic conflicts and tribalism, but never involving murder.

Despite every effort to work as a team, some in the executive committee tried to take sides based on their ethnicity. When I intervened, I was told often that I didn't get it. In other words, I was a foreigner, a stranger to Rwandan issues, and therefore I wasn't the right person to be solving problems in a still bleeding country. I refused to be silenced. Though I didn't know much about Rwandan history, I knew I hadn't been appointed to solve the political issues that had existed long before I was even born.

I understood well my responsibilities before the members of the Pentecostal church, the people of Rwanda, and God.

We came to the end of the one-year term without organizing elections. The government of Rwanda understood our challenges, so we were given six more months to get the work done. In the end, a general meeting was called to elect a permanent executive committee. On December 4, 1997, I was elected Secretary General of the Pentecostal Church of Rwanda. Some Tutsis started to call me Kofi Annan (the Secretary General of the UN at the time) while Hutus called me Paul Kagame (the country's vice-president and Minister of Defence). In 1997, Kagame was still hailed as the strongman of Rwanda who had stopped the genocide and overthrown the Hutu regime. I tried to understand both perceptions of my personality, if not my mission. However, I wasn't happy that fellow Christians were trying to sully my pastoral image.

DRIVEN BY MY VALUES

I was very young and entrusted with big responsibilities. Because I didn't know much about the history of Rwanda, both inside and outside the church, I relied on God's promises to use me during the difficult times. Every time I faced leadership challenges, one name came back to my mind: Joseph, the young Hebrew man. The son of Jacob taught me three things: confidence, faithfulness, and forgiveness.

Regarding confidence, Joseph was the eleventh of the twelve sons of Israel. One day he had a dream that he was predestined to lead his whole family. As a man of faith, he believed that God would fulfil His plan for him. Therefore, he was courageous to affirm his God-given leadership before his brothers first, even though they already hated him, and to his parents. The story unfolds like this:

Now Israel loved Joseph more than any of his other sons, because he had been born to him in his old age; and he made an ornate robe for him. When his brothers saw that their father loved him more than any of them, they hated him and could not speak a kind word to him.

Joseph had a dream, and when he told it to his brothers, they hated him all the more. He said to them, "Listen to this dream I had: We were binding sheaves of grain out in the field when suddenly my sheaf rose and stood upright, while your sheaves gathered around mine and bowed down to it."

His brothers said to him, "Do you intend to reign over us? Will you actually rule us?" And they hated him all the more because of his dream and what he had said.

Then he had another dream, and he told it to his brothers. "Listen," he said, "I had another dream, and this time the sun and moon and eleven stars were bowing down to me."

When he told his father as well as his brothers, his father rebuked him and said, "What is this dream you had? Will your mother and I and your brothers actually come and bow down to the ground before you?" His brothers were jealous of him, but his father kept the matter in mind. (Genesis 37:3–11)

One day the dreamer, as his brothers named him, was sent by his father to go to Shechem to see if all was well with his brothers and with the flocks. Joseph, a young man of seventeen, agreed to undertake a scary sixty-five-mile walk at a time before GPS, when the safety of travellers was uncertain. Just a little while before, there had been bloody fighting between the Israelites and the natives of Shechem (Genesis 34). Joseph was convinced that God had predestined him to a great mission and therefore would protect him against his enemies, including his brothers who hated him. After a few days of searching for his brothers, Joseph didn't find them at Shechem. He decided to walk the extra miles until he found them near Dothan.

At his arrival, his brothers welcomed him with cruel faces despite his caring heart for them. The following scripture describes Joseph's traumatizing moments:

So Joseph went after his brothers and found them near Dothan. But they saw him in the distance, and before he reached them, they plotted to kill him.

"Here comes that dreamer!" they said to each other. "Come now, let's kill him and throw him into one of these cisterns and say that a ferocious animal devoured him. Then we'll see what comes of his dreams."

When Reuben heard this, he tried to rescue him from their hands. "Let's not take his life," he said. "Don't shed any blood. Throw him into this cistern here in the wilderness, but don't lay a hand on him." Reuben said this to rescue him from them and take him back to his father.

So when Joseph came to his brothers, they stripped him of his robe—the ornate robe he was wearing—and they took him and threw him into the cistern. The cistern was empty; there was no water in it.

As they sat down to eat their meal, they looked up and saw a caravan of Ishmaelites coming from Gilead. Their camels were loaded with spices, balm and myrrh, and they were on their way to take them down to Egypt.

Judah said to his brothers, "What will we gain if we kill our brother and cover up his blood? Come, let's sell him to the Ishmaelites and not lay our hands on him;

after all, he is our brother, our own flesh and blood." His brothers agreed.

So when the Midianite merchants came by, his brothers pulled Joseph up out of the cistern and sold him for twenty shekels of silver to the Ishmaelites, who took him to Egypt. (Genesis 37:17–28)

It would be unfair to think Joseph ever forgot the most horrific experience of his lifetime. However, I dare to believe that even in the dry pit and in the hands of a caravan of Ishmaelites, Joseph continued to have confidence that one day he would see God's promise fulfilled.

The same confidence drove Joseph to faithfulness. Genesis 39 tells us that Joseph was taken down to Egypt. Potiphar, one of Pharaoh's officials and the captain of the guard, bought him. Joseph was well-built and handsome, and after a while Potiphar's wife took notice and said, "Come to bed with me!" Joseph refused to engage in an unfaithful solicitation, thus he was put in jail because of the woman's evil plot. From jail, Joseph was elevated to the highest political position in Egypt. Because of his confidence and faithfulness, God made a way where there was no way. Pharaoh put him in charge of the whole land (Genesis 41).

When I grew up, I often heard people say in Swahili, "*Dunia ni kidogo.*" This means that the world is very small. It was said when people met in unexpected places. Maybe someone had done wrong and thought they would hide forever. Or someone did a good thing that deserved a reward, but they could not be found. These days we say that the world has become a global village.

Well, the time soon came when a severe famine hit the land of Canaan. Jacob (Israel) sent his sons to go and look for food in

Egypt. Genesis 42 tells us that when the eleven brothers arrived in Egypt, Joseph recognized them and they did not recognize him. He let them go back to Canaan without telling them who he was. When they came back, Joseph let them go again without revealing himself. Genesis 45 describes Joseph's heart for his brothers during their third trip to Egypt.

> *Then Joseph said to his brothers, "Come close to me." When they had done so, he said, "I am your brother Joseph, the one you sold into Egypt! And now, do not be distressed and do not be angry with yourselves for selling me here, because it was to save lives that God sent me ahead of you.* (Genesis 45:4–5)

Every time I read these powerful words, I am reminded that a heart of forgiveness is the most liberating gift one can ever have. Being stuck in the negative experiences of the past only takes away our peace and the bright future before us. Had Joseph used his influence to get revenge on his enemies, who knows what the future would have brought?

The power of his predestined leadership can be summarized in these few words: *"Come close to me. I am your brother Joseph…"* Surely Joseph never forgot the agony he had gone through a few years earlier. Rather, the conviction of his sacred mission, God's protection throughout his ordeal, and his elevation from the pit to the palace caused him to understand that he was there for his brothers' welfare despite the past.

During my four years as Secretary General, I was motivated by one deep desire: day and night, I meditated on ways to bring true unity to church members across the country. In the beginning, my colleagues and I visited members in local churches almost every week to listen and bring encouragement. Everywhere we visited, we allowed enough time to hold conversations with all the leaders at the provincial and local levels.

There were still ethnic tensions within the church leadership, and sometimes among the leadership and the congregations. For decades, pastors and church employees had been forced to complete identification forms in which they were required to indicate their ethnic group. Therefore, it was not taboo for church members and ministers to raise ethnic issues during our meetings. Ethnic ideology was deeply engraved in the people's minds, inside and outside the church in Rwanda.

As we continued our daily struggles of bringing congregants together, serious allegations overshadowed our efforts. Most Tutsi and moderate Hutu in the church spoke about a political party that was created in October 1993 with the support of the ADEPR executive committee and the Swedish missionaries. Many witnesses in the church said that the political party, Union Social des Démocrates Chrétiens (UNISODEC), was officially launched at the local church of Nyarugenge, Kigali. Other rumours from inside and outside the church alleged that the UNISODEC participated in the genocide. Alison Des Forges writes:

> The director of the CZN in Musebeya was Celestin Mutabaruka, who was president of the Union social des démocrates chrétiens (UNISODEC) political party, a small offshoot of the MRND.[12]

In a footnote, she further explains:

> Mutabaruka was also a fervent member of the Pentecostal church. According to several observers in

---

[12] Alison Des Forges, *Leave None to Tell the Story* (New York, NY: Human Rights Watch, 1999), 317.

the commune, he denied benefits of participation in the project to anyone who was unwilling to join his party and his church.[13]

Though Pentecostals were known to distance themselves from politics, the UNISODEC haunted the ADEPR and its leadership from time to time. I didn't know Mutabaruka personally, because he had fled the country when we arrived in Rwanda, nor did I know anything about the UNISODEC. Every time this issue was brought up, I felt embarrassed and kept quiet.

Besides the ethnic issues, thousands of Tutsis from the exile were in the church. Some pastors and laypersons from the diaspora wanted positions in the church, whether they were qualified or not. Life was difficult for many who had moved to Rwanda, from which their parents had left decades ago. The most challenging issues were housing and employment. This does not include the Tutsi who were marginalized in Rwanda for decades due to their ethnicity.

Moreover, people felt the anger and pain caused by the atrocities of war. Many Tutsis had lost their relatives, women had been raped, and thousands of widows and orphans lived in the country. On the other hand, many Hutus had family members who were killed, thrown in prison, or sent into exile. Also, the Hutus who had fled Rwanda after the genocide were returning from the Congo in great numbers. However, the Tutsis had more power in the army and in all other levels of government. When I had been in the Congo, I had never dealt with such leadership conflicts. I often wondered how unity could ever happen.

---

[13] Ibid.

PAPURO RW'IMYIRONDORO Y'UMUKOZI W'ITORERO
RYA PENTEKOTE RYO MU RWANDA

ITORERO RYA PENTEKOTE RYA *GIHINGA*
AMAZINA Y'UMUKOZI *HAKIZIMANA Paul-Marcel*
IGIHE YAVUKIYE *1958*
AMAZINA YA SE *SEZONGO Francois*
AMAZINA YA NYINA *NYIRAWIDONYE Magdeleine*
UBWOKO *Hutu*
AHO YAVUKIYE *Suki Mayaga* AHO ATUYE *Kayove*
UMULIMO AKORA MW'ITORERO *Umukuru w'Itorero*
AHO AWUKORA *ADEPR GIHINGA*
AMASHULI YIZE *6* ABANZA AYISUMBUYE
AMASHULI YA BIBLIA *26 (ITK Kumara) + Spéciale le'eyradio*
IGIHE YAKILIYE AGAKIZA *1973*
IGIHE YABATILIJWE MU MAZI MENSHI *05/12/1976*
IGIJE YABATILIJWE MU MWUKA WERA *Ukwakira 1980*
IGIHE YATANGILIYE GUKORA UMULIMO WA IMANA *Ngeri 1976*
MBESE YATANGILIYE UMULIMO WA IMANA MW'ITORERO RYA PENTEKOTE ? *YEGO*
NIBA ATALIHO NI HEHE ? YAHAKOZE IMYAKA INGAHE ?
MBESE YIGEZE AHAGALIKWA K'UMULIMO ? CIHE KI ?
IGIHE YASUBILIYE K'UMULIMO ?
AMAZINA Y'UWO BASHAKANYE *Nyirabakiga Camille* IGIHE YAVUKIYE *1960*
IGIHE BASHAKANIYE *20/8/1988* BASHYINGILIWE MW'ITORERO ? *Yego / 20/8/1988*
IRIHE ? *ADEPR GIHINGA* RYALI ? *20/8/1988*
MBESE YARAMUKOYE ? *YEGO* RYARI ? *20/8/1988*
MBESE UMUGORE AFITE NIWE WA MBERE ? *YEGO*
NIBA ATARI WE UNDI YAGIYE HE ?

AMAZINA Y'ABANA N' IGIHE BAVUKIYE

AMAZINA	YAVUTSE KUWA	IGITSINA	ARUBATSE
HAKIZIMANA Melisée	*16/05/1990*	*Hergol*	

Pastor Paul Marcel, a Hutu.
He is still with the ADEPR.

URUPAPURO RW'INYIRONDORO Y'UMUKOZI W'ITORERO
RYA PENTEKOTE RYO MU RWANDA
●●●●●●●●●●●●●●●●

Itorero ITORERO RYA PENTEKOTE RYA. *Rugamba.*

Amazina.... *Gatare   Gaspard*....

Igihe yavukiye........... *1940*..........

Amazina ya se.. *Kakira.... Léopard*......

Amazina ya nyina. *Nyiramakwavu. Anastasie*....

Ubwoko........ *Umututsi*................

Aho yavukiye .. *Baneza*.......... Aho atuyo .. *Rugamba*......

Umwuga – umulimo akora mw'Itorero. *Pasteur*....................

Aho awukora.. *Rugamba*...

Amashuli yize........... Abanza *6e primaire*.. Ayisumbuye. *Rugambo*

Amakuru............

Amashuli ya Biblia ... *3*.................

Igihe yakiriye agakiza........ *1964*..........

Igihe yabatirijwe mu mazi menshi.. *le 31/5/.1964*......

Igihe yabatirijwe mu Mwuka Wera.. *le 23/7/.1966*:....

Igiho yatangiriye gukora umulimo w'Imana.......... *1965*....

Mbese yatangiriye gukora umulimo w'Imana mw'Itorero rya Pentekote? *yee*

Niba atariho ni hehe?..~........... Yahakoze imyaka ingahe? ~.....

Mbese yigeze ahagarikwa ku murimo? *Oya*..... Cihe ki? ~...

Igihe yasubiriye ku murimo? ~....

Amazina y'uwo bashakanye *Mukamazimpaka. Adele*. Igihe yavukiye. *1938*

Igihe bashakaniye........ *1958*.... Bashyingiriwe mw'Itorero? *yee. 1959*

Iriho?. *Eglise de Pentecote*...... Ryari?. *le 26/8/.1969*...

Mbese yaramukoyo?.. *yee*......... Ryari?....... *1966*....

Mbese umugoro afito ni wo wa mbere?. *Oya*........

Niba atari wo undi yagiyo ho?. *Yashatse ahandi*

AMAZINA Y'ABANA N'IGIHE BAVUKIYE

AMAZINA	YAVUTSE KUWA	IGITSINA	ARUBATSE
1. *Uwimana. Marie Stephanie*....	*1960*	..*F*...	*yee*....
2. *Habimana. Jean Pierre*.	*le 31/1/.1963*	..*M*....	*oya*....
3. *Niyitegeka. Nicolas*.	*le 27/9/.1972*.	..*M*....	*oya*....
4...............	....	....	....
5...............	....	....	....
6...............	....	....	....
7...............	....	....	....
8...............	....	....	....
9...............	....	....	....
10..............	....	....	....
11..............	....	....	....
12..............	....	....	....
13..............	....	....	....

N.B. Umuzo kuzuza iyi fishi yohorezanyo n'ifoto 2 za passeporte
tukohororeza carte ywo ikiranga ko uri umukozi w'Itororo rya
Pentekote ryo mu Rwanda.

Pastor Gaspard Gatare was Tutsi.
He was killed with his wife and children during the genocide in 1994.

Our church's president held more power than I did, per the church constitution, and he was a Hutu. We were the two key leaders influencing decisions and resolutions. In the aftermath of the genocide, many Hutu leaders weren't bold enough to confront ethic issues. Some of them were openly accused of supporting the perpetrators of genocide, whether they had been involved or not. In some cases, Tutsis complained about their Hutu pastors and church employees, accusing them of killing Tutsi or assisting the genocidaires. On many occasions, the church president chose to remain indifferent, not wanting to be targeted by either side. Therefore, I often felt a duty to act. In fact, after I realized how deeply ethnicity has infected all Rwandans, I felt constant pressure to act as a mediator. With God's help, I was determined to fight for unity at any cost. I was determined not to be influenced by my ethnicity, regardless what Hutu or Tutsi would think or say about me.

Besides the duty to act, more strategies were needed to rebuild the church and the country. Everyone in the executive committee understood that it was important to implement strategies that would create opportunities for church leaders and congregations to come together and fellowship as brethren despite the scars and wounds of the past.

Due to limited financial means, we put more emphasis on church conventions that brought congregations together. As means became available, we encouraged seminars at all levels: pastors and other church employers, women, youth in general, and students. Later, we launched a literacy program in churches across the country, sometimes using sanctuaries as classrooms until appropriate centres were built for the purpose. Most of the projects we implemented were financed by SIDA (Swedish International Development Cooperation Agency) via PMU

InterLife (the Swedish Pentecostal International Relief and Development Agency).

Another program caught the attention of Rwandans of all ethnic groups, a program through which we encouraged local churches to reach out to prisoners. The message was simple but strong: repentance and forgiveness. Many prisoners had been charged in the genocide, and there was a sentiment in many that they deserved to die and go to hell. This ministry became strong in a few prisons across the country. Many prisoners began to come out and confess their involvement in the genocide, and some were baptized in water after the confession of sins.

While prisoners were being set free spiritually, and certainly they were set free psychologically, some Hutu thought this was a tactic implemented by the Tutsi to infiltrate prisons and facilitate the prosecutors and police in identifying and convicting genocidaires. Also, some Tutsi saw this as an alliance with "demons." Why would anyone in the world baptize a genocidaire? On both sides, I was a manipulator.

By 1999, many people didn't want me in my position of Secretary General, both Hutu and Tutsi. However, it wouldn't be easy for me to go before the end of my four-year term. Thus, a group of pastors, most them Tutsi, made up a plot that would put me in jail. Though I knew people were unhappy with my leadership, I didn't know anything about the plan to get me into trouble.

One day I woke early, as usual, and went to my office. At the end of the day, I went home. After supper, when my family and I were sitting in the living room watching TV, I heard a surprising press release from the government of Rwanda. The press release stated that a cabinet meeting chaired by His Excellency, the President of the Republic, Pasteur Bizimungu had temporarily suspended the ADEPR executive committee. The press release added that the committee members and regional overseers had been invited to meet in one week's time with Anastase Gasana, a minister in the president's office. Our children were too little to understand the seriousness of the announcement, but my wife and I were shaken.

I spent all night asking if anyone else had a clue what was happening. Unfortunately, none of our pastors knew anything. The next morning, I started the day with hope that someone somewhere would tell me something. I went from one ministry office to another, from one police station to another, until someone gave me a copy of a letter signed by a few pastors and the vice-president of a high court, who was also an assistant pastor in one of our churches. The letter was addressed to the President of the Republic, complaining about our leadership. In the letter, the pastors targeted me and Pastor Justin Gasana, a survivor of the genocide and vice-president of the committee, accusing us of supporting a group of Hutu refugees operating outside Rwanda to destabilize the country. These were serious accusations that were enough to have me arrested, given the precarious security issues the country was facing.

One week after the press release, we met with Anastase Gasana. The minister of justice and three other cabinet ministers were also present. Minister Gasana opened the meeting with a short introduction, telling everyone why we were there. Then he called on one of the accusers to say briefly why they had written to His Excellency Pasteur Bizimungu. After the accuser finished, I was given a chance to speak.

My defence was short and simple. I began to remind everyone that I had been born and raised in the Congo and had moved to Rwanda in July 1994, after the genocide. I also brought to the attention of the cabinet ministers that I was a

Tutsi and that I was aware that the Tutsi had significant power in the country, militarily and politically. I then asked everyone how I could be so foolish as to rally behind the people who had lost power, many of them having shed the blood of innocent people.

I explained that there were extremist Tutsi in the church who wanted to see every Hutu in jail. On the other hand, there were extremist Hutu in the church who wished that all Tutsi had died. I concluded by stating that I was a victim of my values, which had always pushed me fight for the unity of all Rwandans, whatever the price. As a final remark, I told everyone that, although I was a Tutsi by birth, I had a pastoral heart that wouldn't let me close my eyes before any injustice.

After I spoke, Minister Gasana asked our legal representative (a Hutu) to speak. In a few words, he said that he was surprised by the accusations and that the accusers weren't trustworthy.

Minister Gasana broke the meeting for a while and all the cabinet ministers withdrew. When they came back, Gasana commended us for our great commitment to the rebuilding of Rwanda. He concluded by saying that the government was behind our leadership, and that the accusations had been dismissed. He also mentioned that we should take disciplinary measures against the pastors who had falsely accused us. The meeting ended with a prayer.

A PRIZE FROM UNESCO

The days that followed were rewarding. We continued our leadership without major opposition in the church. As the days passed, more literacy centres were opened across the country. Young and adults who didn't have chance to go to school were graduating from our literacy centres with skills in writing and reading. We continued to encourage seminars and church conventions at all levels. We implemented programs that brought four hundred thousand church members together. We also undertook the renovation of elementary schools and high schools. Before the end of 2001, we completed the building of a significant hospital in the rural area of Nyamata, a few miles from Kigali. It was officially inaugurated by the President of the Republic, His Excellency Paul Kagame.

By the end of 2001, a major announcement was made by the government of Rwanda. Someone somewhere had been watching our efforts with an appreciative eye. One day while I was sitting in my office, I received a call telling me that ADEPR was a recipient of the UNESCO International Reading Association Literacy Award. I was told that the award was already in the office of the President of the Republic.

Here is the announcement as posted on the UNESCO website:

Meeting from 2 to 6 July 2001 at UNESCO Headquarters in Paris, THE JURY, appointed by the Director-General to award the International Reading Association Literacy Award, the Noma Literacy Prize, the King Sejong Literacy Prizes and the Malcolm Adiseshiah International Literacy Prize in recognition of the services of institutions, organizations or individuals having distinguished themselves by making a particularly meritorious and effective contribution to the struggle against illiteracy,

Recalling that the International Reading Association Literacy Award, the Noma Literacy Prize, the King Sejong Literacy Prizes and the Malcolm Adiseshiah International Literacy Prize were established in 1979, 1980, 1989 and 1998 respectively through the generosity of the International Reading Association, the late Mr Shoichi Noma of Japan and the Governments of the Republic of Korea and India,

Recognizing that the demanding challenges of literacy cannot be met unless the necessary political will and commitment of Member States is aroused, the active participation of intergovernmental and non-governmental organizations, especially those working at the grass-roots level, is ensured and a broad movement of international solidarity is created,

Having examined twenty-seven nominations submitted by governments and one by a non-governmental organization in compliance with the stipulations and criteria of the General Rules Governing the Award of Prizes for Meritorious Work in Literacy, THE JURY has unanimously decided to award…

THE JURY, conscious of the need to reward, make known and encourage the many individuals, projects and activities in the field of literacy that can serve as examples and sources of inspiration, has further unanimously decided to award honourable mentions to the following institutions and organizations:

International Reading Association Literacy Award to the ASSOCIATION DES ÉGLISES DE PENTECÔTE DU RWANDA, RWANDESE REPUBLIC, for: (1) making its first priority the struggle against illiteracy within the framework of its welfare and sociocultural programme and persevering with literacy work under extremely difficult circumstances and despite limited financial resources; (2) reconstructing literacy centres in several provinces and establishing pilot literacy centres in Kigali town, rural Kigali and Gitarama; (3)

introducing new and more efficient methodology and training of literacy educators; and (4) integrating national reconciliation with the literacy programme as well as with the struggle against sexually transmitted diseases and the AIDS pandemic.[14]

The award was celebrated by the government of Rwanda in August 2001 on the International Women's Day.

LEAVING RWANDA

The recognition of our efforts by UNESCO and the Rwandan government encouraged me and everyone in the executive committee. Our efforts were also celebrated by Pentecostal churches across the country.

However, we were almost at the end of our four-year term and a general meeting was about to be called to elect a new executive committee. As the day of the decisive meeting approached, another group of pastors arose to oppose my candidacy, but they failed. At the general meeting held in Kigali on March 6–7, 2002, I was re-elected to the position of Secretary General for another term of four years.

A few months later, the opposition against my leadership intensified. Some of these pastors had come from the diaspora, while others were survivors of the genocide and wanted positions in the church. Because they were Tutsi, they thought I should back them up whether they were right or not. Our legal representative, who had more power than I did as per our constitution, chose to remain indifferent. I was the scapegoat.

My dear pastors did everything to shake me. In the end, they made up another serious case against me. This time they planned to betray me using ethnicity. It was a time when

[14] *UNESCO*, "Literary Prizes." Date of access: November 17, 2016 (http://www.unesco.org/education/literacy_2001/en_lit_prizes.shtml).

Rwanda was threatened by the neighbouring Uganda, following confrontations between the two countries a few years earlier in the Congo. Most of us thought Uganda might launch an attack on Rwanda.

The pastors knew that I had been born in the Congo near the Ugandan border. My mom had died in 1988, six years before we moved to Rwanda. None of the pastors who accused me knew my mother, but maybe they knew that I had ties with Uganda through my mother's family. Given my position, they made the case that I was a serious threat to the security of Rwanda because of my ethnicity.

They associated me with a well-known Ugandan politician, Mr. Mateke, who was from a district that bordered with the Congo. They circulated false information in the security services and among top politicians that my father had been a Hutu from Uganda and a relative of Mateke. Two people with different sources warned me about potential harm. I was targeted with one threat after another by people within the church.

With the deep conviction that my mission was over for the time being, I decided to leave Rwanda, leaving behind a legacy that will be remembered even when I'm gone: the legacy of audacity, the legacy of unity.

Chapter Seven

NEW
LIFE IN NORTH AMERICA

MY ARRIVAL IN THE UNITED STATES

While I was facing the most troubling tests of my leadership, I received prophetic messages from different men and women saying that I was going to continue my ministry in another country. One of the messages said clearly that God was going to send me to a country with people of a different colour. The woman who brought me that message in 2001 added that God was sending someone with a paper I needed for my journey. I didn't understand the message at the time.

One Saturday in July 2002, I awoke in the middle of the night, my thoughts wandering here and there. Before I fell back asleep, I decided to get up early and attend a service in the local church of Gisenyi.

When dawn broke, I took a shower and left. While on my way to Gisenyi, I made a phone call to let the senior pastor know I was coming to join them for the morning service. I don't remember exactly what his reaction was. Usually, if I planned to visit a local church, I had to let them know a few days ahead of time. Otherwise someone could think I had a hidden agenda.

At the end of the service, the senior pastor introduced me to his guest, for whom he had prepared a delicious African meal. He was an American man in his fifties. We had a good conversation in the pastor's house. At the end, we exchanged mobile telephone numbers, and I invited him to have a meal with me when he returned to Kigali. His name was Cleveland. That day, I left Gisenyi and went back to Kigali not knowing that this man had been sent to help me get the paper I needed to travel to North America.

A few days later, Cleveland called me to let me know he was back from Gisenyi. We arranged to have dinner. In the evening, we enjoyed grilled chicken accompanied with grilled green bananas and other appetizers. As we ate, enjoying the fresh air, he began to talk about African American life in the United States.

"Pastor, I have visited many countries in West Africa because I thought that's where my ancestors came from," he said. "But I never felt that I belonged to any of the countries I visited. Now, I feel like my sister must be somewhere in Rwanda."

I knew he was joking. I then told him that the king of Rwanda had refused to sell his people for slavery, and that he had fought the Europeans when they tried to take his people by force.

I do not recall how we ended the conversation, except that Cleveland invited me to visit him in the United States. I told him that if I ever got an American visa, I would visit him.

The following week, Cleveland called me while I was on a trip to Cyangugu. I was driving and the whole executive committee was with me. Because my English was not as good as today, I hardly understood Cleveland's talk of the papers he had dropped by my office. I told him that I would look at them when I returned.

When I returned to my office, my secretary gave me an application form for an American visa. I called Cleveland and asked him what he wanted me to do with the papers. He told me to fill them out and take them to the American embassy near my office. He said that he had already spoken with the woman in charge of visa applications and that she would issue me a visa.

I filled out the application form over the next few days, collecting the required documents. I then took the application to the embassy in the morning of July 18, 2002. The woman in charge of visa went through my application and said that I was missing a letter of invitation. I told her that I had been invited by Cleveland. She understood, and then told me to come back in the afternoon.

I returned to my office with no hope of getting a visa. Two years prior, I had been invited to come to Canada by Justin Rees, the President of the Upstream Christian Initiatives in Abbotsford, British Columbia. However, the Canadian embassy in Nairobi had refused me the visa. I thought that since Canada had refused me, I wouldn't obtain one from the United States either.

I went back to the American embassy in the afternoon to find many people lined up and waiting to hear if they would be issued a visa. When my turn came, the embassy official gave me my passport with a ten-year visa with multiple entries. As soon as I saw it, my brain reminded me about the woman who had told me that God would send someone with a paper I needed for my journey.

In the first week of October 2002, I left Rwanda with my wife and our five children. The family stayed behind in Uganda while I flew to New York on October 20. It was my first trip to North America. My English was very poor, and the few words I knew were difficult for Americans to understand. I was alone with no friends or anyone to help me find a place to spend that first night.

Before we landed, I connected with a man from Uganda who promised to help me find a motel. But I lost track of him as everyone passed through immigration and never found him again. The airport was so huge; I didn't know which direction to take. But after I got my luggage, I followed the crowd and finally found myself outside.

They were many taxis, but I hesitated to take one because I didn't know where to go. Because of my English, I felt nervous asking for help. As I stood outside, I saw a young black man coming towards me. As he came closer, he seemed to realize that I needed him. He stopped and asked if I needed help. When we started to speak, he noticed that I had difficulty speaking English. He then asked me where I was from and I told him I was from Rwanda. He was from Congo Brazzaville.

My heart jumped. I realized that God had sent an angel to help me. We then began to speak in French. I told him that this was my first visit to the United States and that I didn't have a place to sleep. He asked me if I had money to book a hotel, and I said yes. He offered to help me. He put my bag in the taxi he was driving and we left.

As we headed downtown, he stopped by a McDonald's and bought me a cup of coffee. He then drove me to a motel near Central Park and helped me to book a room. I paid him a few dollars and he left. Unfortunately I didn't get his contact information in case I needed him later.

I spent almost three months in New York. In the end, I decided to travel to Montreal in Canada because I was so frustrated by American English. I knew that Montreal was French, and I already had a few Rwandan contacts living in Montreal and Toronto.

In January 2003, I left New York for Montreal.

LIFE IN CANADA

When I left New York, it was already winter. It was cold compared to Rwanda, but bearable. As soon as I arrived in Montreal, the weather was different. It was so cold, far beyond my expectation, and there was a lot of snow everywhere. My first impression was that life couldn't be better in such weather. For the first few weeks, I wondered why I had come to suffer in the cold. I was also troubled by my separation with my wife and children. Back in Africa, I had only ever left my family for a few days at a time when we visited churches. In 2001, I had spent one month in Europe during a visit to Sweden, Belgium, and France.

As my lonely life went on in Canada, I became more sensitive to children left without parents, and widows who had never imagined that war and genocide would one day separate them from their loved ones. I became more aware that widows and orphans don't only suffer psychological and emotional pain, but they also lack food, clothing, and medicine. Charity organizations may help, but they're not there all the time for every need.

Thus, I knew my family was struggling, and moreover, they needed my financial support. My family joined me eight years later. Despite the immigration challenges, I worked and sent money to my wife regularly, whether she asked for it or not. When I arrived in Canada, we had agreed that she would look after our children, and I assured her that I would work hard to supply every need they had. I understood from the beginning that it wasn't easy for her to work and look after five little ones in a foreign country. Every time my wife or children called asking for money, seeking attention, complaining, or telling me stories, I thought of the widows and orphans. On several occasions, after hanging up the phone, my heart went back to Rwanda and those widows and orphans I hadn't been able to help.

Immaculée and the children alone in Kampala, Uganda.

My life continued in Montreal and I didn't know when my family would join me. After one year in the largest francophone city of Canada, I decided to move to a place where I could learn English. I knew God had put before me an open door for ministry, so I thought I would be limiting myself if I continued to speak only French and other African languages.

In January 2004, I moved to Edmonton. In those days, it was easy to find employment there. During my first job interview, I didn't understand everything the boss asked me, and she noticed that I had trouble with the language, but she still hired me. She probably understood that I was educated, and she gave me a chance to learn while working. Thus began my life in Alberta, struggling with English and the anxiety caused by my separation from my family.

Besides getting a job, I had another priority: to find a Pentecostal church I could call home. It didn't take long to find Gospel Centre Pentecostal Church, where I attended until the end of 2012. The congregation was almost ninety percent Caucasian. My first months there were mixed with comfort and confusion. From the first Sunday, I felt at home. That day, Reverend Murray Coughlan gave a sermon that encouraged me. I came back every Sunday until I decided to stay.

After a few months, I had made many friends among the congregation. The only thing I missed was the warmth and friendliness of my brothers and sisters back home. Although these new friends were sensitive to my situation and assisted me in many ways, I sometimes felt as if they were helping me out of pity.

In African Pentecostal churches, when the service was over, people hugged one another and didn't rush to get home. Church life continued throughout the week, not just on Sundays. The congregants visited one another and called one another whenever possible. A church was a true family.

After a couple years, I understood that Canadians were more reserved inside and outside the church. One day during a men's ministry session, we were told to make small groups and share our struggles. In the small group, a man said, "Before you open the door, you have to know who is behind it." That meant a lot to me.

During the eight and a half years I spent at Gospel Centre, I appreciated the humble and caring heart of my pastor, Murray

Coughlan. Whenever I needed him, he was there. Whenever I needed something, I got it.

Immaculée in Kampala (2004).

Though it is true that Canadians are more reserved, they are models of human rights. This is real at the bus station, in the grocery store, in hospitals, in government services, almost everywhere. People respect one another, and if something needs to be fixed, they fix it in a polite way. Sometimes unfair treatment happens, but it's not in the Canadian culture to close one's eyes to injustice. Despite the cold weather and culture shock struggles, this makes immigrants proud.

My life in Canada continued without my family for such a long time. I continued my work as a happy man, smiling all the time as if everything was all right. Behind my smile I hid my great frustration and anxiety. But it didn't prevent me from meeting people and having fun.

In Edmonton, when I met new people, they wanted to know my origin. Thus, I introduced myself by giving my first name. In Canada, my name sounds funny to many, Innocent.

A few months after I arrived in Edmonton, I was waiting for a bus. It was early morning in the winter. A young Caucasian girl came to me at the bus stop and wanted to ask me about the bus schedule.

"Hi," she said to me.

"Hi," I replied. "I am Innocent."

That's just a polite Canadian way to introduce yourself to someone new.

"I'm not harassing you," she immediately said, misunderstanding me.

"Oh! I mean, my name is Innocent."

"Really?" she said. "Nice to meet you."

I smiled. "Nice to meet you."

On another occasion, I met the director of human resources of the agency I worked at for nine years. He was supposed to know my name, but for some reason when I greeted him, he looked at me strangely. It was a Christmas party where clients, staff, and management met to share a meal. When I saw the human resources director walking in, I welcomed him.

"I am Innocent," I said as usual.

He looked at me, gestured wildly, and walked away. I understood that he thought I was joking.

Such incidents happened often. Finally, I searched the origin of my name. Surprisingly, I found this:

> From the Late Latin name Innocentius which was
> derived from innocens... This was the name of several
> early saints. It was also borne by thirteen Catholic
> popes including Innocent III, a politically powerful
> ruler and organizer of the Fourth Crusade.[15]

After this discovery, I understood that some people are more informed than others. The only person who wasn't surprised by my name was a Catholic priest I met in Edmonton. When I introduced myself to him, he said, "Oh! Saint Innocent!" And then he spoke about the Catholic Pope Innocent. He knew it because he had learned about the Catholic popes and saints.

Besides my name, almost every time I meet a new person, they ask me the common question: "Where are you from?" For those who aren't familiar with Canada, I belong to a group of people called the "visible minority." Statistics Canada describes the visible minority as "persons who are non-Caucasian in race or non-white in colour and who do not report being Aboriginal."[16] The category includes Chinese, South Asian, Black, Filipino, Latin American, Southeast Asian, Arab, West Asian, Korean and Japanese.

Therefore, every time I told someone I was from Rwanda, I got an answer like this: "Yeah, I watched Hotel Rwanda. It was horrible" or "I can't imagine how human beings can do such horrible things" or "Where were you at that time?" But the question that embarrassed me most was "Are you Hutu or Tutsi?" Sometimes I answered, "We don't talk about those things. I am Rwandan." Every time I gave such answer, I felt

---

[15] *Behind the Name*, "Innocent." Date of access: November 17, 2016 (http://www.behindthename.com/name/innocent).

[16] *Statistics Canada*, "Classification of visible minority." Date of access: November 18, 2016 (http://www.statcan.gc.ca/eng/concepts/definitions/minority01a).

like I was trying to pretend that ethnic groups don't exist in Rwanda.

I have learned how people can miss certain things not because they are ignorant, but because they haven't heard or learned about them.

A few years ago, my church invited a guest to speak on the Jewish Passover and the Christian Easter. He was a Christian Jew. After the service, I approached him and introduced myself. After mentioning that I had come to Canada from Rwanda, I spoke a bit about the genocide. Then I told him that some people think Tutsi have Jewish roots and that the Tutsi and Jewish genocides are the worst in the twentieth century because they share blood. When I asked him if he had ever heard this, he changed the subject.

"You know, throughout history Tutsi are known as brave worriers," he said. "After they killed a Hutu president, Hutu did not have another choice but to defend themselves by killing the Tutsi." He continued to convince me that Hutu were extremely angry, and that their anger had been provoked by the Tutsi who had killed their president. This Jewish preacher concluded that because Hutu were extremely angry, it was understandable that they had killed the Tutsi.

After he had finished speaking, I thanked him politely as many Canadians would, and I walked away. Later I wanted to go back and ask him if the Jewish genocide was understandable, but I chose to contain my frustration.

This preacher wasn't the only person who thought the Tutsi were responsible for their own misfortune. There are many in Rwanda, Africa, and around the world who have the same opinion.

Another incident happened at my workplace. A co-worker from Sierra Leone, who had been newly hired, came to me and asked where I was from. When I told him, he asked if I was

Hutu or Tutsi. He then started a long speech how the Tutsi had killed a Hutu president, and that the Hutu had done the right thing to revenge their president.

I simply asked him how long he had been in Canada, and answered a few months. I then told him that I understood his African way of thinking, and I walked away. For many Africans, a president belongs to his tribe or ethnic group, protects his tribe or ethnic group, and lives and dies for his tribe or ethnic group.

However, in developed countries, a president or prime minister is elected by people to serve the entire nation. While the death of President Habyarimana cost about a million innocent people, the death of President John Kennedy in the United States didn't cost a single life. Being in Canada not only made me feel safe and respected after so many years of humiliation in Africa, but I became more aware that the Hutu-Tutsi conflicts went beyond East and Central Africa. It is up to us, Hutu and Tutsi, to change our history. We can, and we will.

MY FAMILY AND MINISTRY

In the book of Ecclesiastes, Solomon, the son of David and the king in Jerusalem, wrote a poem to remind us that there is a time for everything:

> There is a time for everything,
> and a season for every activity under the heavens:
> a time to be born and a time to die,
> a time to plant and a time to uproot,
> a time to kill and a time to heal,
> a time to tear down and a time to build,
> a time to weep and a time to laugh,
> a time to mourn and a time to dance,
> a time to scatter stones and a time to gather them,

a time to embrace and a time to refrain from embracing,
a time to search and a time to give up,
a time to keep and a time to throw away,
a time to tear and a time to mend,
a time to be silent and a time to speak,
a time to love and a time to hate,
a time for war and a time for peace. (Ecc. 3:1-8)

I often read and preach these words, and I thought I understood them. One of many challenges for pastors, preachers, and counsellors is applying professional principles and rules when addressing a serious issue. Professionalism can sometimes be insufficient. It's not easy to understand someone sitting before us for counselling unless we have gone down the same path they have. When I left my family in Uganda in October 2002, I thought they would join me in a few months. However, it took eight and a half years for my family to join me in Canada. During the wait, I better understood King Solomon's words of wisdom. There is a time for everything, a time to weep and a time to laugh.

My family arrived in Canada on February 11, 2011. On that winter day, I arrived early at Edmonton's international airport with dozens of people from Gospel Centre. There were blacks, whites, Asians, young, and adults, all waiting for my family. As soon as they arrived, my wife rushed to hug me. We hugged one another, and we almost forgot that our children were awaiting my hug, too. She finally released me and I hugged my three daughters and two sons, one after another. We spent a few minutes inside the airport, because everyone who had come from Gospel Centre wanted to speak to my wife. Her English wasn't so good, but she wasn't shy with strangers so she continued talk, and talk, and talk.

It was already late at night, at least for me, but to my family it felt like morning due to the jetlag. In the end, I signalled the people who had come to welcome my family that it was time to leave. I then drove my family in a minivan I had bought four years earlier, knowing they would come soon.

When we arrived home, a three-bedroom apartment on the fourth floor, we took time to thank God for His protection and for reuniting us. I don't remember everything we talked about that night, but one memory will always stay with me. In 2002, before we had left Rwanda, we prayed with a friend named Jacques. During this prayer time, Jacques told us what God had told him; he had seen me in another country, where my family joined me later. He said that he saw my family joining me in a multi-storey building. Prior to coming to Canada, we had never lived in a multi-storey building. Apartments weren't popular in Rwanda or the Congo.

For a couple of days following my family's arrival, we spoke about God's timing. God had known in advance that it would take almost nine years before they joined me in Edmonton, in an apartment on the fourth floor. Now, the time to weep was gone, and it was time to laugh.

I spent one week with my family before going back to work. Every day I made breakfast, lunch, and dinner for them. Afterward, the honeymoon ended and my wife took over. However, I still prepare meals for the family when she needs a break. Many African men don't cook; they say it's a women job!

Seven months after my family joined me, I mustered the courage to complete my Bible studies at Vanguard College. I knew that my decision to pursue education would come with serious financial challenges, but I told my family that God, who had provided for them during the years of separation, would still provide for us. I started school in September 2011 planning to complete my program in April 2013.

Innocent ordination: The Pentecostal Assemblies of Canada (2013)

While I waited for my graduation, my wife and I felt the calling to plant a new church in Edmonton. We had our first meeting in our basement in December 2012. We were nine people: my wife, our five children, and two other ladies. On March 24, 2013, we officially launched the church in a hotel room we rented for our Sunday services. From that time until now, my wife and our five children have taken the lead in the ministry. They are always there in the choir and worship team. They are always there early Sunday morning to set up music instruments, and they are always there to put them away at the end of the service. They are always there to contribute financially in times of need, in the church and in the family. I am extremely proud of my family. Despite the years of separation, God had kept His promise to send us to serve him in another country, with people of a different colour.

The Sezibera family in Edmonton (2016).

Having in mind the reason why my family had come to Canada, I took the time to think of a name for our church. Many names came to my mind, but I was convinced that God wanted me to continue my mission of reconciliation. Thus, we called the church Goshen Christian Assembly. According to the Bible, Goshen was a district in Egypt where the Israelites lived until the exodus. They lived there about 450 years. That's where they were welcomed by Joseph, the brother they had once attempted to kill. Because of Joseph, his siblings came together, worked hand in hand, and became stronger.

> *Now the Israelites settled in Egypt in the region of Goshen. They acquired property there and were fruitful and increased greatly in number.* (Genesis 47:27)

God was with His chosen people in the land of Goshen.

Chapter Eight

SUNSHINE
OVER THE LAND OF A THOUSAND HILLS

THE SUN HAS COME

Jacob, the patriarch of the Jews, was the son of Isaac and Rebekah, and Abraham's grandson. He was the younger twin brother of Esau. When Isaac was very old and couldn't see, Jacob and Rebekah plotted to take Esau's firstborn rights. Rebekah meticulously planned to have Jacob impersonate Esau to fool his father Isaac so that he would bless him. They managed to trick Isaac, but the consequences still remained.

His fear and guilt caused him to leave his family. He fled to Haran, where he lived in his uncle's household for twenty years. Jacob then described the ordeal he had endured while staying with his uncle:

> *This was my situation: The heat consumed me in the daytime and the cold at night, and sleep fled from my eyes. It was like this for the twenty years I was in your household.* (Genesis 31:40–41)

Fortunately, twenty years of pain brought him to reconcile with his brother Esau, whose firstborn rights he had stolen.

Years later, Jacob left Canaan, his home country, for the second time and moved to Egypt with his household. His beloved son Joseph was second only to Pharaoh. For several years, Jacob had believed Joseph had been killed by a ferocious animal, and finally they were to be reunited in Egypt.

The time finally came for Joseph to take his father to Pharaoh. The next words captivated my spirit:

> *Then Joseph brought his father Jacob in and presented him before Pharaoh. After Jacob blessed Pharaoh, Pharaoh asked him, "How old are you?"*
>
> *And Jacob said to Pharaoh, "The years of my pilgrimage are a hundred and thirty. My years have been few and difficult, and they do not equal the years of the pilgrimage of my fathers."* (Genesis 47:7–9)

After two decades of asylum to his uncle Laban, and after making every effort to form a comprehensive and honest reconciliation with his brother Esau, Jacob was still hurt by the past. He had never lived the happy life he'd anticipated when he planned and executed his mother's malicious plan to trick Isaac. A lifetime of 130 years was summarized in one short sentence: *"My years have been few and difficult."* In comparing his longevity to that of his father Isaac and grandfather Abraham, maybe he also remembered how faithfully his fellow patriarchs had walked before God and men during their long lives in this deceitful world.

I dare to believe that there is no political solution that will erase the memories and pain caused by the 1994 genocide of the Tutsi. I still think of my parents who died natural deaths—my mother in 1988, my father in 1998—and later my older sister died in 2006. Although I hope to see them again, before that bright day I will always remember them. How about those who don't know how their family members died, or those who witnessed their gruesome deaths? Can any politician, psychologist, counsellor, or pastor help them to forget? Only the Creator can heal the broken-hearted and bind up their wounds (Psalm 147:3).

When I arrived in Rwanda in July 1994, only three months after the genocide, I didn't think that one day I would be happy to live there. Corpses were scattered everywhere in the country, and houses were abandoned, many of them destroyed, especially houses belonging to the Tutsi. Most of the cities smelled of death and uncertainty.

When I was still in the Congo, I once came across a dead body near a river. I was terrified. Almost three decades later, I still remember that river and the body lying on the bank, though I'll never knew who the person was. How can a survivor of genocide forget? How can those innocent people—Tutsi and Hutu, children, adults, men, and women—forget what their eyes have seen? The survivors of genocide live daily with wounds and atrocious memories.

On the other hand, it would be unfair to forget the pain of millions of Hutu in Rwanda, Burundi and the Congo who, one way or another, were affected by the past. While Tutsi were being killed, it is reported that Hutus died in great numbers in Burundi in 1972. Many more fled to neighbouring countries, especially Rwanda and Tanzania. Then, decades later, the Tutsi of Burundi were killed en masse. Between 1990–1994, it is reported that many Hutus were killed by the war between the RPF and the defeated government. It would be unfair and unwise to ignore the wounds and the scars of the Hutu orphans, widows, and refugees. As President Barack Obama said once, "The best history helps us examine mistakes"[17] We can dismiss the truth in our daily talks and politics, but the reality is that the human brains keep a record of all good and bad memories until the last breath.

Today Rwanda has achieved the unimaginable in rebuilding itself two decades after its deterioration. In 1994, the country was almost dead economically. Government offices, commercial buildings, and residential houses were destroyed. The social fabric was in tatters. The beautiful country of a thousand hills was reduced to ash. As the government made efforts to clean the country of the corpses that lay in streets and in houses, while renovating government offices, many of us didn't see better days ahead.

Patricia Crisafulli and Andrea Redmond describe the dark days of Rwanda:

On July 4, 1994, the RPF reached its goal and captured Kigali. Two weeks later, a transitional government was in place. Although the genocide had finally ended, Rwanda was still dangerous, with insurgency and threats against the newly established order. During and after the war, a French buffet area within the country, known as the Turquoise Zone, had become a haven for former genocidaires. From the protection of the zone, these perpetrators fled to Zaire, which is now known as the Democratic Republic of the Congo (DRC), after the conflict. The devastation of the country was so great, and the legacy of the genocide so traumatic, that the country was "widely considered as an irremediable

---

[17] Spoken during a speech at the inauguration of the National Museum of African-American History and Culture, September 25, 2016.

failed state… A staggering number of people were dead, and hundreds of thousands were directly culpable. "This created a profoundly shattered social fabric: 75 percent of the Tutsi population inside the country had been killed, as well as the vast majority of the moderate political and civic voices… From havens in eastern Congo, the former genocidaires continued to wage assaults on Rwanda… Immediately after the war, however, the new political leadership needed to deal with the crushing aftermath. A million people had been killed. Two million lived outside the borders of the country. As some refugees returned, others fled in fear of what might come next.[18]

That was the Rwanda I saw in 1994. The Rwandan leadership has overcome great mountains since then, and it would be unfair not to acknowledge the courage and sacrifice of President Kagame and his team. The question is how Rwanda will look like after Kagame? Will Kagame's children and grandchildren flee Rwanda again? Will they be killed because of their ethnicity? Will my children, despite their Canadian citizenship, fear Rwanda because of their facial features? Will sons and daughters of Hutu be killed because of their ethnicity one day? We all have a responsibility to act. There will always be agents of destruction among us, but let us all rise and say with Nelson Mandela: "A man who takes away another man's freedom is a prisoner of hatred, he is locked behind the bars of prejudice and narrow-mindedness."[19]

---

[18] Patricia Crisafulli and Andrea Redmond, *Rwanda, Inc.: How a Devastated Nation Became an Economic Model for the Developing World* (New York, NY: Palgrave Macmillan, 2012), 66–67.

[19] Nelson Mandela, *Long Walk to Freedom* (New York, NY: Back Bay Books, 1995), 624.

I have quoted a few writers on the origin of Hutu-Tutsi conflicts. We can blame them on the former colonizers again and again, but that's the past. The present and the future are in our hands. Hutu and Tutsi will always live alongside one another in the land of the great lakes. Therefore, it is imperative that we do whatever it takes to cultivate a sustainable peace for our generation, for our sons and daughters, and for the generations to come. That's the will of God, before whom we are all accountable.

While I was working on this book, I learned about a story that moved me. Between 1997 and 2002, I drove by the Catholic church in Nyange and learned about a Catholic priest by the name Seromba. When the priest heard that President Habyarimana had been killed in a plane crash, he encouraged the Tutsi from his parish to hide in his church. Thousands of Tutsi came to find a safe place. Afterwards, bulldozers arrived, pushed in the church, and killed two thousand Tutsi.

That was in 1994. Three years later, a different story occurred in the same place.

Unfortunately, we often focus on negative experiences, the good ones being forgotten. Despite the fact that I'd driven by the Nyange Secondary School, I never heard about what happened there on March 18, 1997. A well-known Canadian travel writer and novelist, Will Ferguson, tells the story:

> On March 18, 1997, when students at Nyange Secondary, having gathered for an evening prep class, heard gunshots nearby, they assumed it was RPF soldiers and Hutu Power rebels exchanging fire… They didn't realize it was their own school that was under attack, or that they themselves had been targeted. Nyange, you see, was a mixed school. Hutus and Tutsis

were all welcome, and the two sides got on well... Men armed with grenades and automatic weapons slipped through nearby Mukura Forest and fell upon Nyange Secondary School, killing the night watchman and storming a classroom, shouting for the students to segregate themselves. "We want the Tutsi on the left, Hutus on the right!" they yelled. The students knew what that meant. No one said a word, so the armed men repeated their command. "Hutus on the right, Tutsis on the left!" A Grade 12 student, Marie-Chantal Mujawamahoro, stood up. Speaking on behalf of her classmates, she replied to the gunmen with a single forceful word: "No." No? Their attackers were taken aback by this. What do you mean, no? No, she said quietly. "We won't do it. There are no Hutus or Tutsis here. We are all Rwandans." The other students agreed, murmuring the same answer. "We are all Rwandans." So the gunmen dragged one of their classmates from the crowd, a girl named Seraphine, who by chance came from a Tutsi family. They killed Seraphine in front of her classmates and then repeated their demand, screaming now: "We know there are Tutsis among you! Divide yourselves! Hutus on the right, Tutsis on the left." Again the students refused. "We won't do it, Marie-Chantal yelled back... The gunmen shot another student... Flustered and livid, and not knowing who were Tutsis and who were Hutus, the men attacked indiscriminately, lobbing a grenade into the classroom from outside and then firing on the wounded through the smoke... These students remind us that the older animosity is generational...[20]

---

[20] Will Ferguson, *Road Trip Rwanda: A Journey into the Heart of Africa* (Toronto, ON: Penguin Group, 2015), 207–209.

This is one story among many telling how the young generation of both Hutu and Tutsi are ready to turn back from the old animosity. We adults, especially parents and leaders at all levels, might model this bright future hovering over the horizon.

LET YOUR LIGHT SHINE

Time and again I have read the book *Shake Hands with the Devil*. I have tried to penetrate the author's heart to understand these words:

> Several times in this book I have asked the question, "Are we all human, or are some more human than others?" ...The only conclusion I can reach is that we are in desperate need of a transfusion of humanity... this new century must become the Century of Humanity, when we as human beings rise above race, creed, colour, religion and national self-interest and put the good of humanity above the good of our own tribe. For the sake of the children and of our future.[21]

I came to my own conclusion that the author, Lieutenant General Romeo Dallaire, is appealing to us as preachers of the good news. Whoever claims to be a minister of God's word should know this: God has committed to us the message of reconciliation.

> *So from now on we regard no one from a worldly point of view. Though we once regarded Christ in this way, we do so no longer. Therefore, if anyone is in Christ, the new creation has come: The old has gone, the new is here! All*

[21] Romeo Dallaire, *Shake Hands with the Devil: The Failure of Humanity in Rwanda* (Toronto, ON: Vintage Canada, 2004), 522.

this is from God, who reconciled us to himself through Christ and gave us the ministry of reconciliation: that God was reconciling the world to himself in Christ, not counting people's sins against them. And he has committed to us the message of reconciliation. We are therefore Christ's ambassadors, as though God were making his appeal through us. We implore you on Christ's behalf: Be reconciled to God. (2 Corinthians 5:16–20)

Jesus Christ Himself is our peace. He has made the two groups one and has destroyed the barrier, the dividing wall of hostility (Ephesians 2:14). This is the reason that the Church exists in this darkest world.

After all, we Christians are the light of the world (Matthew 5:14–16). This well-known scripture has been preached in every church since the first century. So far, since independence, the top leaders of Rwanda, Burundi, and the Congo have claimed to be Christians. Also, most inhabitants of these three countries profess to be Christians. Why then is our region still covered by the darkness of ethnic hostilities? We need to ask ourselves whether we are still on Christ's mission or serving our own self-interests.

Ethnicity is not a curse. I am proud to be born Tutsi, and Hutus should be proud of their ethnicity too. However, my ethnicity doesn't make me who I am. Rather, my personality has been shaped by my faith in Jesus Christ and my daily efforts to be transformed into His image. Ministers of God's word have a sacred mission to reconcile the people of the world with God. And once we are reconciled with our Creator, we will be reconciled with our brethren, despite our ethnicity and the colour of our skin. The day that all preachers of the good news in Rwanda, Burundi, and the Congo stand together as one for the message of reconciliation is the day we will build our legacy.

The students of Nyange Secondary School, some having witnessed the horrors of the twentieth century, have a worldview that should inspire our generation and the generations to come. Someone once summarized the millennial worldview this way:

> A commitment to the common good over individual gain; an ethos that reaches across traditional divisions such as race, ideology, and partisanship. The Millennials are not a "Generation Me" but rather a "Generation We." They are strongly progressive, socially tolerant, environmentally conscious, peace-loving, … They volunteer in record numbers and declare themselves ready to sacrifice their self-interest for the greater good. They do not fit neatly into any classic ideological category and are clearly eager to establish a new paradigm.[22]

This worldview fits the millennials in North America, Europe, and Africa, in cities and towns, and at Nyange Secondary School.

As to our political leaders in the African Great Lakes region, they have a God-given mission to work for the peace of His precious people. After all, God is the One who changes times and seasons; He deposes kings and raises up others (Daniel 2:21), and one day He will bring every deed to judgment with no favouritism to anyone's status. In the same way, the leaders of the most powerful countries in the world—and the United Nations, whenever possible—should not protect their own interests by sitting and watching men, women, and powerless

---

[22] *Small Precautions*, "The Millennial Worldview." November 26, 2008 (http://smallprecautions.blogspot.ca/2008/11/millennial-worldview.html).

children be killed because of ethnicity or religion. In the case of Rwanda, Burundi, and the Congo, the international community should be aware that the Hutu-Tutsi conflict is generational and cannot be solved in one day. Therefore, any effort for peace and reconciliation should be strongly supported.

I dream of a time when Hutus and Tutsis will live beyond the past, casting no suspicious gazes towards one another. That time will come, and we, and our sons and daughters, will live with no more prejudice and fear.

Let us all arise and sing together in unison King David's psalm:

> *How good and pleasant it is when God's people live together in unity! It is like precious oil poured on the head, running down on the beard, running down on Aaron's beard, down on the collar of his robe. It is as if the dew of Hermon were falling on Mount Zion. For there the Lord bestows his blessing, even life forevermore.* (Psalm 133:1–3)

May God bless those who love peace!